101

WAYS TO BUILD A STRONGER, MORE EXCITING

MARRIAGE

H. NORMAN WRIGHT

HARVEST HOUSE PUBLISHERS
EUGENE, OREGON

Cover photo © 4x6 / iStock
Cover Design by Dugan Design Group, Bloomington, Minnesota

101 WAYS TO BUILD A STRONGER, MORE EXCITING MARRIAGE
Copyright © 2014 H. Norman Wright
Published by Harvest House Publishers
Eugene, Oregon 97402
www.harvesthousepublishers.com

Library of Congress Cataloging-in-Publication Data
    Wright, H. Norman.
    101 ways to build a stronger, more exciting marriage / H. Norman Wright.
        pages cm
    ISBN 978-0-7369-6127-1 (pbk.)
    ISBN 978-0-7369-6128-8 (eBook)
    1. Marriage--Religious aspects—Christianity. I. Title. II. Title: One hundred one ways to build a stronger, more exciting marriage. III. Title: One hundred and one ways to build a stronger, more exciting marriage.
    BV835.W733 2014
    248.8'44—dc23

                                                                            2014011077

Printed in the United States of America

            14 15 16 17 18 19 20 21 22 / VP-JH / 10 9 8 7 6 5 4 3 2 1

Contents

Your Marriage Can Be Better Than Ever!

Welcome to a journey—a marriage-enrichment journey. The questions and brief comments are designed to help your relationship grow, improve, and be even more satisfying and fulfilling. And hopefully your partner and you will also grow personally and spiritually as well.

Marriage is the most powerful of all relationships. You and your spouse will either enhance and give the glory to the other or steal the glory of the other. Are you enhancing the glory in your spouse?[1] Can you think of ways to do this? Most of us have never thought about this. Look at your partner. What do you see? Do you see the glory of God residing in him or her? Do you see a unique reflection of God? If not, take a closer look.

As a married couple, you both can encourage and shape the glory of God in the other as no other person can. Enjoy the reflection of God's glory in your spouse. Honor it. Enhance it.[2]

What does this mean? Your marriage relationship comes with a challenge—to take the raw material you each have and work toward revealing more of the glory of God in each other. That's a far cry from what most of us are focused on. But this is what marriage is all about. It's not a time to just kick back and expect to be waited on or catered to. And your marriage isn't just going to "happen" and thrive. For a successful and vibrant marriage, each of you needs to take an attitude of allowing yourself to be stretched.

You are called to *create*, so create. How? By serving, loving, and living out God's Word in ways that build up your spouse. Glorify God by drawing the *best* out of your spouse. Go for the excellent instead of focusing on the not-so-great. Find the rich treasure God has placed in your partner. There is untapped, undeveloped potential in your spouse that, with your help, can surface and grow even more.

Today we hear way too much about marriages that are in trouble or don't make it. Yet there are many, many couples who have fulfilling and even exceptional marriages. It's no accident that strong marriages are the way they are. Good marriages don't just happen. Couples in exceptional marriage are willing to learn and grow by developing a positive, biblical attitude; discovering how to speak their spouse's personal and love languages; and celebrating their differences as well as their similarities.

Does an "absolute formula" exist that couples today can follow to guarantee achieving the marriages they want? You already know the answer to that question. There isn't. But there are principles that have worked for many. Consider the questions in this book as a personal consultation with the nation's leading authorities on what makes marriages work.

Although this book will help and possibly act in place of going to a marriage seminar or a series of counseling sessions, don't expect numerous stories or clever examples. The information you'll find here is bottom line and straight to the point. Because the questions are designed to help you think, share, and grow, they will require some effort on both your parts. And whatever you learn, you need to apply or it won't do any good. These principles and guidelines have made a positive difference for so many couples, and they can also work for you.

Marriage is a lifelong adventure. Every journey has its highs, lows, and detours. And every love journey is unique. No two couples experience the same road. Many couples experience their marriages without giving them much thought, while others constantly take their marital temperature. Some underrate marriage and choose to see problems that aren't there. Others view marriage with blinders on and are oblivious to issues that eat away at the core of their union until it's too late. Which of these descriptions do you connect with?

Think of it this way. Your marriage is like a car. Every now and then it needs a tune-up. Often when your car is receiving a tune-up, the mechanic may find the beginning of a problem and take corrective action. This minimizes the damage. However, if you neglect this service, something may break, resulting in the need for a major overhaul. And that's more expensive, time-consuming, and disruptive. It's the same when you assess your marriage. You may discover the slight fraying of some wire insulation that may eventually cause a short circuit and fry the engine that makes your union work. But discovering it early gives you a head start on taking corrective action.

Commit to spending time each day or each week to connect via this book. Make a determination to read, contemplate, and answer each question. You may not like some of the questions or your spouse's answers, but reflect on them rather than react. Discuss your answers openly and sincerely. Remember that the advice in this book comes from many people who are specialists in the relationship field. Be hopeful. You can grow, and so can your spouse. Your marriage can be better than ever. Each day consider these Scriptures:

> [The LORD says,] "Call to me and I will answer you and tell you great and unsearchable things you do not know" (Jeremiah 33:3).

> "For I know the plans I have for you," declares the LORD, "plans to prosper you and not to harm you, plans to give you hope and a future" (29:11).

1   Safe Haven

Let's consider your marriage in a new way. Do you feel safe? Do you feel valued? Is there a better way to resolve your disagreements? Drs. Archibald Hart and Sharon Hart Morris have provided key insights in their book *Safe Haven Marriage—Building a Relationship You Want to Come Home To*. Let's consider what they wrote:

> The image of a safe haven, a place that protects us from the raging seas of life, is a metaphor for what every marriage should become. All couples, when they marry, look forward to seeing their relationship become a haven for their hearts.
>
> Marital partners yearn for their spouse to see them for who they are and to be there for them. Spouses want to be fully understood, accepted, and valued by their mates.[1]
>
> Can you envision a marriage in which you would feel safe enough to say what you feel? In which you were assured that your spouse would respect, or at least attempt to understand, your point of view? Under those circumstances, at the end of an argument you could come back together and reestablish your emotional warmth.[2]

❖ In the midst of fighting and arguing that goes on between you and your spouse, what do you each long for?

❖ Are you a safe haven for your spouse's heart? Do the things you say and do reflect that?[3]

2 Emotional Disconnect

Emotions are a foundation for marriage. They involve the care of a relationship. When we experience emotional wounding, we become cautious and even distant. Consider these insights:

> Emotional disconnection doesn't require an emotional earthquake. Just pile on the critical comments, insensitive remarks, and irritating acts, whether intentional or unintentional, and you can break your partner's heart. Not much more than a flat-toned hello from your spouse after you've waited all day to see him, a kiss that did not seem warm, a hand touched then quickly pulled away, unwillingness to stop for a hug, failure to help get the kids up and ready in time for school, the thoughtlessness of not putting the dishes in the sink, clothes left in the hallway, or not having time to listen when a listening ear is desperately needed—all these can do damage, one bit at a time.[4]

> Creating and sustaining an emotional connection with your spouse is the most important goal of your marriage. Once that connection is in place, neither the busyness of life, past hurts and disappointments, perceived betrayals, nor differences in family background and lifestyle will have the power to do serious damage to your safe haven.[5]

❖ When are the times you feel emotionally connected with your partner?

❖ When do you feel emotionally disconnected?

3   Winters and Summers

Let's get a bit historical about your marriage. It helps to see where you've been. On a piece of paper, draw a time line of your marital relationship. What were the early years in your marriage like? Over the years of your marriage, when were the good seasons and when were the rough seasons? Place a "W" next to the years that were difficult (your "winters") and an "S" next to the years that were warm and good (your "summers").

❖ What events or seasons in your marriage defined your marriage as a safe haven?

❖ What events or seasons in your marriage tried to redefine it as an unsafe place for your heart?[6]

4 Your Attachment

From early in our lives until the day we die, we ask our loved ones, "Can I trust you to be emotionally available, accessible, and responsive when I need you?" Our parents were our earliest mirrors, reflecting back to us our worth and meaning. Then came other family members and relationships with friends and acquaintances across our life span.

Not having someone who was a good, truthful mirror early in life can severely damage the way we love in later relationships. Everyone comes to marriage with preset beliefs, expectations, values, and feelings pertaining to these crucial issues:

- Expectations of what real intimacy looks like.
- Ways of responding to hurt, disconnection, and disappointment.
- A sense of being unlovable or unworthy, questioning whether you are able to obtain easily and comfortably the love you need from others.
- A sense of the emotional safety or non-safety of others; questioning if others can be trusted to love and take care of your heart.[7]

❖ Describe your expectations of intimacy.

❖ Give examples of how you respond to hurt, disconnection, and disappointment.

❖ Give examples of how your spouse responds to hurt, disconnection, and disappointment.

❖ Do you feel you get enough of the love you need? Explain.

❖ Do you trust others with your heart?

❖ Do the following descriptions of a "securely attached couple" fit your relationship? If not, what can you do at this time to improve?

> Securely attached couples are able to:
>
> - Hold on to a deep sense that they are loved and valuable
> - Know from experience that their spouse is trust-worthy and will be loving, supportive, and responsive
> - Understand, make sense of, and express their emotions appropriately
> - Share their needs and hurts and reach out for others
> - Make sense out of fights and get back on track when the fight is over
> - Emotionally connect during and after fights[8]

5   Arguments

Do you ever argue? Need I even ask the question? Everyone argues at times. It's how arguments are handled and ended that can create problems.

❖ In your relationship, what often triggers arguments?

> What turns an innocent conversation, a quiet stroll, a guileless comment, or a team effort in the kitchen into an argument? It seems that a conversation is always one sentence and one emotion away from turning into an argument. It is often the case that arguments start when one spouse is hurt because he feels unseen, misunderstood, and devalued.
>
> There are four events that make a spouse feel his or her partner wasn't there for them.[9]
>
> - First is *criticism*. Critical remarks feel like put-downs. They devalue us.
> - Second is a *demand* (or request) that is perceived as unfair and unreasonable. Your spouse asks you to do something that you don't want to do because you feel it doesn't make sense.
> - Third, conflicts are also triggered by what are called *cumulative aggravations*. These are annoying, frustrating things that one's spouse does repeatedly and over time.
> - A fourth trigger is *rejection*. A partner's failure to

respond in a caring and considerate manner can feel like rejection.[10]

❖ What is your experience when you sense the start of an argument?

❖ To get a picture of the cycle of your arguments, complete these statements:

- Our usual arguments start when...
- I respond by...
- And then you...
- I then...
- And you then...
- We come together and emotionally connect by...

❖ Think back to your last several arguments. What did you hope would be the outcome?[11]

6   Losses in Marriage

When you marry, you gain a lot. I'm sure you're aware of that. But you also give up some things. What did you give up? Well, is your marriage everything you wanted it to be? Probably not. There were and are losses we experience when we marry. That's why the glue of marriage is "commitment." It's doubtful that you've talked about the things you "lost" after you married, but they're there. We all have expectations and dreams that are unfulfilled. We become aware of what we don't have rather than what we do have. What are the choices we have when it comes to realizing our marital losses?

- Some people want out of their marriages.
- Some become stuck.
- Some change their expectations.
- Some change the situation.
- Some actively grieve their losses.

Discuss the following questions suggested by Dr. Scott Stanley.

❖ Are there significant areas in your marriage where you have a sense of loss? What are they?

❖ Talk about your expectations related to areas of sadness, loss, or frustration in your marriage. What is reasonable? What is not reasonable?[12]

What can you do when it comes to losses? Focus on changing your own expectations. Together, read these two passages and discuss what they mean for your marriage.

If it is possible, as far as it depends on you, live at peace with everyone (Romans 12:18).

Why do you look at the speck of sawdust in your brother's eye and pay no attention to the plank in your own eye? How can you say to your brother, "Brother, let me take the speck out of your eye," when you yourself fail to see the plank in your own eye? You hypocrite, first take the plank out of your eye, and then you will see clearly to remove the speck from your brother's eye (Luke 6:41-42).

Grieve over your losses. Say goodbye to them and let them go. It may help to grieve together. Read and learn as much as you can about grief since you both will experience losses throughout your marital journey.[13]

Suggested Reading

H. Norman Wright, *Experiencing Grief* (Nashville: Broadman & Holman, 2004).

H. Norman Wright, *Recovering from the Losses in Life* (Old Tappan, NJ: Fleming H. Revell, 1991).

Scott Stanley, PhD, *The Heart of Commitment* (Nashville: Thomas Nelson, 1996), chapter 4.

7 Ups & Downs

Think about this insight from Dr. Scott Stanley:

> I believe there are some telling similarities between marriage and the stock market. Marriage is a great long-term investment. Satisfaction in marriage, however, goes up and down all the time, kind of like the Dow Jones industrial average—a major indicator of how the market is doing. Some stocks see fewer bumps and dips than others. Some days and months see less ups and downs. Same for marriages. The "happiness rating" in some marriages has more volatility than others. Some couples bounce around a lot more than others in terms of satisfaction. Either way, the long-term view of commitment carries you through ups and downs in marital happiness over many years. Investing in marriage is like investing in the stock market in that while it may be one of the best bets over the long term, it is also risky. You are not guaranteed that your investment will yield the return you are hoping for. Some people have suffered significant losses in their marriages. But, by far, most who consistently invest in their marriages will do very well in life.[14]

❖ How are you doing at making regular investments in your marriage? What things do you do that you consider investments (large and small)?

❖ What kind of investments do you appreciate most from your partner?

❖ What kind of investments does your partner appreciate most from you?

❖ What specific investments will each of you try to increase in your marriage?[15]

8 Giver/Taker

❖ In your relationship, which person is more of a giver?

❖ In your relationship, which person is more of a taker?

Do you think those are strange questions? They aren't. They're important questions. We live in a culture that focuses on self or "me." Often this is carried into our marriages, and so we focus on "what I want, what I can get, and what my partner can give me." Selfishness lives in all our marriages to some degree, but it needs to be given an eviction notice. If you want your marriage to be unfulfilling, you give to yourself.

Think about these two verses:

> Let no one seek his own, but each one the other's well-being (1 Corinthians 10:24 NKJV).

> Let each of you look out not only for his own interests, but also for the interests of others (Philippians 2:4 NKJV).

❖ In what ways do you see yourself putting into practice these two passages?

❖ Ask your spouse for a specific way you can be more of a giver in your relationship.

❖ In what ways do you work together as a team?

❖ When do you work best as a team?

❖ What are the ways your spouse gives to you?

❖ What does the following passage say to you and your marriage?

> The fruit of the Spirit is love, joy, peace, forbearance, kindness, goodness, faithfulness, gentleness and self-control. Against such things there is no law. Those who belong to Christ Jesus have crucified the flesh with its passions and desires (Galatians 5:22-24).

9   Other People in Your Marriage

What about other people in your marriage? You know—children, in-laws, other relatives, friends, coworkers. How are your boundaries? Gregory Popcak, in his book *The Exceptional Seven Percent— The Nine Secrets of the World's Happiest Couples*, suggested:

> Boundaries protect the dignity of the person, the importance of the marital imperative, and the intimacy of the marriage over all other relationships. When a person is unable to set appropriate boundaries, she experiences a great deal of confusion and stress as all the people she knows and roles she occupies compete to receive the lion's share of her time and energy.
>
> Every day is a new opportunity to renew your wedding vows. When you give your mate his or her good morning kiss, I would encourage you to tell your mate (or at least think to yourself), "Today, I'm going to say, 'I do' all over again, by considering our marriage in every choice I make."[16]

Let's consider your boundaries in three areas: work, friendships, and relatives.

Work Boundaries Quiz

T   F   I feel more rewarded by my work than I do my marriage and family life.

T   F   I am often thinking about work when I'm home.

T   F   My spouse and I regularly argue about our work schedules.

T   F   I use my job as a way of escaping the craziness of my home life.

T   F   I regularly have to break dates with my spouse or miss family events due to my work.[17]

Friendship Boundaries Quiz

T   F   I have one or more friends who are constantly in crisis and I always feel obliged to run to their aid.

T   F   My spouse complains about the amount of time I spend with my friends.

T   F   I think of my friends as the people I go out with to escape the craziness of my marriage or family life.

T   F   I tell my friends things I would never tell my mate.

T   F   I feel closer to some of my friends than I do my spouse.[18]

"Family of Origin" Boundaries Quiz

T   F   I often feel torn between my mate and my parents.

T   F   There are no secrets between my parents and me. I tell them everything that goes on between my spouse and me.

T   F   I probably spend more time with my parents than with my mate.

T   F   My mate complains about the amount of involvement my parents have in our lives.

T   F   I feel too guilty to ever say "no" to my parents.[19]

10   Gratitude

❖ What does the word "gratitude" mean to you?

❖ What are the expressions of gratitude you give to your spouse?

❖ What expressions of gratitude does your spouse give to you?

Catch Your Mate Being Good

It is all too easy to focus on the things we don't like about our mates, especially when we are irritated with them. Everyone loves approval, but husbands and wives tend to be more stingy with it than they should be. As a result, spouses end up feeling unappreciated by and isolated from each other. So why not keep a *Gratitude Journal*?

Every night before bed, sit together as a couple and write down or discuss the things your mate did for you or was to you for which you are grateful that day. These will primarily be simple things, such as giving a compliment or helping defuse a situation with the children. This will remind you of all the little ways you take care of each other.[20]

Look for Growth Opportunities

While no spouse wants his or her mate to have short-comings, the fact is, we all do. Even if we are working to overcome them, from time to time our partners are going to stumble into our flaws and vice versa. In such times, it is a very mature spouse who can see the opportunity for growth these situations present for him- or herself.[21]

Keeping a Balanced View

The exceptional spouse's job is to keep both sides of his or her partner's qualities in mind. This way, even when you feel the need to address a particular irritating trait, you can remain grateful for your spouse's good points, and approach your mate in a more respectful way.[22]

11   Diminishing Love

"Diminishing love." Have you heard this expression? Probably not, but you've more than likely heard "I fell out of love." Well, how do you fall out of something like that?

❖ My definition of love is...

❖ My spouse's definition of love is...

❖ What are several reasons people fall out of love?

One of the leading counselors on this subject is Michele Weiner-Davis. Consider her words:

> First of all, people don't just *fall* out of love. If love dwindles, it's because the marriage wasn't a priority. Love is a living thing. If you nurture it, it grows. If you neglect it, it dies.
>
> The number one cause for the breakdown in marriages in our country is that people don't spend enough time together. They take their marriages and their spouses for granted.
>
> Second, love isn't just a feeling, it's a decision. Happily married people understand that if they engage in activities that bring love into the marriage, they will *feel* loving. There is no magic or mystery here. What you decide to do on a daily basis will determine how much love you and your partner feel for each other.
>
> To have a loving marriage, you have to put yourself out and love your partner the way he or she wants to be loved.[23]

Remember, the love that is needed to stabilize a marriage is the type of love God displays to each of us—unconditional commitment to an imperfect person.[24]

12   Are You a Cheerleader?

We like cheerleaders. They encourage us because they believe in us. They motivate us. In marriage, it's all too easy to let this quality die out. Consider the following questions.

❖ In what way would you say your spouse is a cheerleader toward you? How does he or she encourage you?

❖ In what way would you say you are a cheerleader to your spouse? How do you encourage him or her?

❖ How would you like to be encouraged?

We live in a mistake-oriented culture. Would your spouse say you are equipped to point out mistakes, weaknesses, and liabilities rather than strengths? Your answer speaks volumes about the tone in your marriage.

When you're an encourager, you're like a prospector or a deep-sea diver looking for hidden treasure. Every spouse has pockets of underdeveloped resources within him- or herself. Your task is to search for those pockets, uncover and display them, and then work to enhance them. As you discover the strengths in your spouse, you'll begin to focus on them more and more. Be a cheerleader!

13 What Does and Doesn't Work

Isn't it interesting that we tend to spend more time and effort focusing on what doesn't work than what does—even in our marriage relationships? Think about this, and then share your responses to these questions.

❖ What is different about the times you get along great?
(What are you doing? What are you saying?)

❖ What have you done in the last year that has made your marriage more fulfilling?

❖ What can you accomplish this week that will build up your marriage? (Make sure you choose something that is possible and attainable.)

The next time something negative comes up about your marriage, notice what's different about the times it's there but something constructive happens.

❖ How do your conflicts usually end? (What brings them to a halt? Who says and does what?)

This week why not do something different? Sit down each night and predict whether the next day will be a good day or a bad day. At the end of the next day, share your perception—whether the day went well or not. [25]

❖ Did how you approach the day make it more positive?

In *Why Marriages Succeed or Fail*, John Gottman, PhD, suggests that a key ingredient in stable marriages is the negative and positive responses between husband and wife. If the ratio is five to one in favor of positive responses, he concludes that the marriage, despite the couple's possibly differing communication styles, tends to be stable.[26] What are some positive responses? They include showing interest, having a listening ear, affection, thoughtfulness, appreciation, concern, empathy, acceptance, laughter, and joy.[27]

If research indicates these are determining factors of marital stability, then assisting couples to learn to develop their positive responses may create solutions for problem behaviors. There are also biblical teachings that tell us we need to overcome negativity and sin through positive behaviors. Read these passages out loud together and then discuss them.

> I, therefore, the prisoner for the Lord, appeal to and beg you to walk (lead a life) worthy of the [divine] calling to which you have been called [with behavior that is a credit to the summons to God's service, living as becomes you] with complete lowliness of mind (humility) and meekness (unselfishness, gentleness, mildness), with patience, bearing with one another and making allowances because you love one another (Ephesians 4:1-2 AMP, brackets in original).

> Be kind and compassionate to one another, forgiving each other, just as in Christ God forgave you (4:32).

> As God's chosen people, holy and dearly loved, clothe yourselves with compassion, kindness, humility, gentleness and patience. Bear with each other and forgive one another if any of you has a grievance against someone. Forgive as the Lord forgave you. And over all these virtues put on love, which binds them all together in perfect unity. Let the peace of Christ rule

in your hearts, since as members of one body you were called to peace. And be thankful (Colossians 3:12-15).

❖ How do you see yourself putting these passages into practice in your marriage?

14 Sex

How easy is it to let a vital part of marriage become routine? The busy pace and multiple distractions of our lives tend to interfere with our sexual expression. Is a clean house really more important than a romantic sexual encounter? Is one more appointment at the office a valid trade-off for time together in bed? Is the last hour of TV a valued substitute for physical enjoyment? Are you unconsciously collaborating to avoid sex?

I encourage you to make your sexual experience a marital priority and leap the hurdles to achieve that together. You and your partner need to decide your unique style in making sure both your sexual needs are being met. Preplanned "love appointments" need not take the fun, excitement, and even the spontaneity out of making love.

Sexual touching is a vital part of a husband–wife relationship. As with other forms of marital communication, touching does take time and effort as you discover and continue to explore what works best for your partner and you.

You will differ in your desire for expressing physical love. To increase the enjoyment of physical touching in your marriage, evaluate your present experiences. After each of you have completed the following statements, share your responses with one another.

❖ Some of the ways I like to be touched are…

❖ Some of the ways I don't like to be touched are…

❖ I think my partner likes to be touched…

❖ The times I like to be touched are…

❖ The times I prefer not to be touched are…

❖ I think we touch each other this many times a day:

❖ Who does the most touching in our relationship?

❖ Who prefers to do the touching in our relationship?

❖ When I am touched, I feel…

❖ When you are touched, you feel…

❖ The way we could improve our touching is to…[28]

15   Married to Me

This will be a hard question because it takes extreme honesty on your part to answer. This is not a question to ask your spouse. Each one of you needs to answer the question separately, and then share your responses with one another. Here it is…

❖ What is it like being married to me?

Be honest. Be open. Give some thought to this. And then share the information with your spouse.

Now, after you've each shared your response, ask each other the next important question.

❖ In what area(s) would you like to see me make some improvements?

No matter what your spouse says or what you hear, respond with, "Thank you for letting me know."

Each person in a marriage needs to take an attitude of allowing him or herself to be stretched. You're called by God to grow in ways you may never have dreamed of. So make the decision to develop competence in areas in which you were previously uninterested or untalented. Take the risk of trying something new. And if you fall flat on your face, get up and try again. Everyone has a learning curve.

You want to seek ways to better serve your spouse, to make his or her life easier, and to better meet his or her needs. Your calling in marriage is not to dump your responsibilities onto your spouse and make his or her life and workload heavier. Your calling is to reach into your spouse's life and lighten his or her life and load.

16 Dream On

Take a few minutes to think about the following questions, and then write down your responses.

❖ What was the dream you had for your marriage?

❖ What have you done to make this a reality?

Now discuss your answers.

Most couples have dreams for their marriage, and that's good. Dreams pull you, prompt you, drive you, and give you hope. You need to dream, and dreaming big is great if it's realistic.

Unfortunately, over the years I've heard too many couples say, "Give up your dreams for marriage. If you don't, you'll only be disappointed. Accept what happens and what you get." How pessimistic and fatalistic.

I wish more couples were made up of dreamers. That way they would see their marriages as they *could* be. To see only what is—and, therefore, to settle for marital mediocrity or give up on it entirely—is contrary to what God wants for your marriage. His calling is not just for you to stay married but for you to both work together to develop an exciting, vibrant relationship that reflects His ongoing presence. And that kind of marriage will be fulfilling!

So dream…dream on! Dream realistically and dream big.

17 Vision

"Vision." It's an interesting and important word and concept for marriage. Some couples spend their marital journey drifting. Others are purposeful. What is the vision you have for your marriage for the next year? What is your vision for your marriage five years from now? Perhaps you've never thought about this, but now is the time to discuss it.

Unless you have a clear and precise understanding of where you're heading in your marriage, the probability of a successful journey is limited. Proverbs 29:18 (kjv) is a statement that is foundational for a successful marriage: "Where there is no vision, the people perish." A paraphrase of this is "Where there is no vision, a marriage relationship stops growing and begins to crumble."

Having a vision for your marriage is having a realistic dream for what your spouse, you, and your marriage can become under God's direction.

❖ What does God want for your marriage?

Without God's wisdom and guidance, anything you might achieve in your marriage might be out of His will and not good for your union in the long run. "The Lord knows all human plans; he knows that they are futile" (Psalm 94:11).

18 Transitions

From birth until death, life is a series of transitions. A transition is a bridge between two stages of life. In between there can be a time of uncertainty. One stage terminates and a new one begins. As you know, any new change carries an element of risk, insecurity, and vulnerability—even change that is predictable and expected. Every transition carries with it seeds for growth, new insights, refinement, and understanding. But in the midst of turmoil, sometimes the positive aspects seem too far in the future to be very real. There is also a sense of loss that may or may not be recognized or acknowledged.

Some people wish life were like a DVD player. Whenever they find a particular stage that is especially satisfying, they want to hit the pause button and remain there awhile.

- ❖ Which transitions in your life have given you the greatest sense of joy? Explain.

- ❖ Which transitions have given you the greatest sense of loss? Explain.

- ❖ What transitions in your spouse's life gave him or her the greatest sense of joy?

- ❖ Which transitions have given your spouse the greatest sense of loss?

- ❖ What transitions might you personally experience in the next five years?

- ❖ How do you think they will affect your partner and your marriage?

- ❖ What can you do now to prepare for the transitions?

Where do you go from here? People who make positive transitions face life and prepare in advance. They are able to adjust and sort out which crisis needs to be handled first.

19   Know Your Spouse

How well do you know your spouse? Think about this before you answer. Some couples are strangers to some degree. Why? They don't pay attention to the details of some aspects of their spouse's life. The more details (even seemingly insignificant ones) you know about your spouse, the closer you will feel to him or her. Couples who know more about each other's worlds handle stress and conflict better.

Answer the following questions and then share your responses. You may want to ask each other the questions.

By giving honest answers to the following questions, you will get a sense of the quality of your current relationship. For the most accurate reading of how your marriage is doing, both of you should complete the following.

How Well Do You Know Your Spouse Quiz

T   F   I can name my partner's best friend.

T   F   I know the names of some of the people who have been irritating my partner lately.

T   F   I can tell you some of my partner's life dreams.

T   F   I can list the relatives my partner likes the least.

T   F   My partner knows my favorite music.

T   F   I can list my partner's three favorite movies.

T   F   My spouse is familiar with my current stresses.

T   F   I know the three most special times in my part-ner's life.

T   F   I know my partner's major current worries.

T   F   I know what my partner would want to do if he or she suddenly won the lottery.[29]

So, what did you learn about your partner?

20 Problems

Adversity and problems are part of life. "Beloved, do not think it strange concerning the fiery trial which is to try you, as though some strange thing happened to you" (1 Peter 4:12 NKJV). The Message paraphrase puts this verse in a unique way: "Friends, when life gets really difficult, don't jump to the conclusion that God isn't on the job. Instead, be glad that you are in the very thick of what Christ experienced. This is a spiritual refining process, with glory just around the corner."

It's during times of trials that we grow and develop our character. Answer each of the following questions. Perhaps you've discussed these before, but today focus on what you may not have shared with your spouse.

* What difficult events or periods have you gone through?

* Are there any significant psychological insults and injuries you've sustained? Explain.

* What are your losses, disappointments, trials, and tribulations?

* What have you learned through experiencing these?

21 All You're Meant to Be

One of the purposes of marriage is for you to become all you were meant to be. Another purpose of marriage is for your spouse to become all he or she was meant to be. Marriage can take you to a new level if you allow it to and if you let God mold and reframe you according to His Word and His desire. Consider and discuss these questions.

❖ What are the deep traumas or crises you've undergone as a child or adult?

❖ How did you survive those events?

❖ What are their lasting effects on you?

❖ How did you grow emotionally and spiritually?

❖ How do these events and the way you protected yourself and were healed affect your marriage today?

❖ Describe the person you want to become and how you can attain it.

❖ How can your spouse help you in this journey?

Do you reflect much about your life or your marriage? Are you aware of what "reflection" means? Actually, reflecting on something is bending it back to take a closer look. It involves thinking. It involves meditating. It's asking questions of yourself about thoughts, beliefs, values, identity, goals, and, most of all, who God created you to be and wants you to be. When you reflect, you see the real you.

❖ Describe a special moment you've had with a family member.

❖ If you had 100 days of life left, how would you use them?

❖ What would you say is sacred in your life?

You're called to reflect on your life so you can discover what's sacred and realize it doesn't change no matter where you are along life's path…even in your marriage.

23   Your Calling

According to God's Word, your calling, your spouse's calling, my calling—every Christian's calling—is to love one another, including spouse, children, relatives, friends, and even the "unlovable." A friend suggested these thoughts:

> So it's the end of the day, and each of us is lying in our bed reflecting. Have I loved well? Has love been the beating heart pushing through all my activities? Can it be heard in all my conversations? Seen in my eyes? Felt when other people are in my presence? Was the truth I spoke today spoken in love? Were the decisions I made today based on love? Were my reactions? My devotions?
>
> Have I loved well?
>
> If we can answer yes to that [last] question, it is enough.
>
> It may not be enough for our employer...[for] our fellow workers...[for] all the carpools and committees and other things on our calendar.
>
> It may not even be enough for us.
>
> But it is enough for God.
>
> And that should make it enough for us.[30]

❖ What can you do now to ensure that you love well?

❖ What can you do now to ensure that you love well within your marriage?

24   Lessons Learned

What are the major lessons you've learned that you can share with others? Mature people develop the habit of extracting lessons from everyday experiences. Here are a few questions to jog your memory and get you started.

❖ What has God taught you about failure?

❖ What has God taught you from lack of money?

❖ What has God taught you from pain or sorrow or depression?

❖ What has God taught you through waiting?

❖ What has God taught you through illness?

❖ What has God taught you from disappointment?

❖ What have you learned from your family, your church, your relationships, your participation in small groups, and your critics?

> Your life message includes sharing your godly passions. God is a passionate God. He passionately *loves* some things and passionately *hates* other things. As you grow closer to him, he will give you a passion for something he cares about deeply so you can be a spokesman for him in the world.[31]

❖ How are you caring about what God cares about?

❖ What have you learned and done so far that is your primary life message?

Remember, God can speak to others through your life if you let Him.

25 Communication

How's the communication between your partner and you? I mean, how is it *really*? Communication is to love what blood is to your body. No blood—no life. Let's take a closer look at your communication. Take your time on this section—even a couple of days or more. It's that vital.

❖ Share your definitions of communication with one another and discuss the differences.

Set a date with your mate for sharing your responses to the questions that follow in this section.

Use an X to indicate your level of communication, with 1 meaning almost never, 2 meaning rarely, 3 meaning sometimes, 4 meaning often, and 5 meaning almost always. Use a circle to indicate what you think your spouse's level of communication is at the present time.

Set 1

1. Listens when the other person is talking

    1   2   3   4   5

2. Appears to understand spouse when he or she shares

    1   2   3   4   5

3. Tends to amplify and say too much

    1   2   3   4   5

4. Tends to condense and say too little

    1   2   3   4   5

5. Tends to be critical or nag

    1   2   3   4   5

6. Encourages spouse

    1   2   3   4   5

7. Tends to withdraw when confronted

    1   2   3   4   5

8. Holds in hurts and becomes resentful

    1   2   3   4   5

9. Lets spouse have say without interrupting

    1   2   3   4   5

10. Remains silent for long periods of time when the other is angry

    1   2   3   4   5

Set 2

1. Fears expressing disagreement if the other becomes angry

    1   2   3   4   5

2. Expresses appreciation for what is done most of the time

    1   2   3   4   5

3. Complains that the other person doesn't understand him or her

    1   2   3   4   5

4. Can disagree without losing his or her temper

    1   2   3   4   5

5. Tends to monopolize the conversation

    1   2   3   4   5

6. Feels free to discuss sex openly with spouse

    1   2   3   4   5

7. Gives compliments and says nice comments to spouse

   1   2   3   4   5

8. Feels misunderstood by spouse

   1   2   3   4   5

When you get together to discuss your responses, be sure to follow these positive communication guidelines:

1. Set a time and select a place where there are no interruptions from people, phones, etc.

2. Hold your spouse's hand (this helps keep a lid on emotions).

3. Begin by sharing how you scored yourself. If any statement in the first set had a level 3 or lower, or if any statement in the second set had a score of 3 or higher, state your intentions for improving in this area.

4. After you've both shared your scores, continue to hold your spouse's hand and share the scores that reflect how you see one another. Don't say "You do this" or "You don't do this" but, rather, "This is my perspective" or "This is the way I see the situation." For any statement in the first set with a level of 3 or lower, or for any statement in the second set with a level of 3 or higher, say, "I would really appreciate it if you would work on this."

5. When your spouse shares how he or she sees you and makes a request, do not be defensive, point out an exception, or blame the other. Just say, "Thank you for sharing your perspective. I'd like to think about that." You're not agreeing with your spouse or admitting he or she is correct. You're just considering his or her view.

❖ In what ways is your spouse the right one for you to have married?

Think about it and talk about it. After that continue reading.

Marital happiness depends little on the person you marry. At first we were concerned about meeting the "right one" to marry. Now we are learning how important it is to *be* the "right one" for someone else.[32]

If you treat the wrong person like the right person, you could have married the right person after all. On the other hand, if you treat the right person like the wrong person, you most likely married the wrong person. I also know that it is far more important to be your spouse's right person than it is to marry the right person. In short, whether you married the right or wrong person is primarily up to you. How you treat your partner is what makes all the difference. That's worth thinking about.

In one sense, we all choose the "wrong person" to marry because there's something wrong with all of us. We are created in God's image, but at the same time we are afflicted with the same fatal condition caused by the fall of man in the garden. The idea that we are born sinful has become politically incorrect, but the evidence is too strong to ignore. We are flawed. We are broken. We are all wrong people.

27 Sexuality

Cliff and Joyce Penner developed the following discussion tool for couples so that you can increase your understanding and enjoyment of your sexual relationship. Think about your responses before speaking them, hold hands with your spouse, and share.

- I like to initiate.
- I like making love in the morning.
- Direct initiation is the most positive for me.
- I like to have sex several times per week.
- I like our lovemaking experiences to be different every time.
- I look forward to a lot of excitement and creativity.
- For me there is a strong connection between my sexuality and my spirituality.
- I like my spouse to initiate.
- I like making love at night.
- I like subtle initiation.
- I have little need for talking…before making love.
- I have little need for talking during making love.
- I have little need for talking after making love.
- I like subtle and indirect sexual talk.
- I have no need to talk about it later.
- I like the lights off.
- I like predictability.

❖ Share any other thoughts you have on sexuality within your marriage.[33]

28   Embracing Similarities and Differences

❖ What are four ways you are similar to your spouse?

❖ What are four ways you are different from your spouse?

❖ In what ways do your similarities and your differences
   enrich your marriage?

❖ Have you ever considered that in some ways you married a
   "foreigner"?

Think about this: How similar or different your spouse and you
are in personality does *not* affect the success of your marriage. Your
success in marriage depends on how you *handle* your differences
and similarities. Everyone marries a "foreigner" to some degree.
Even if you married someone from the same cultural background
or neighborhood, the longer you're married, the more differences
you'll discover in preferences, ways of doing things, speech patterns,
explaining what you mean, and so forth. All of these can result in
major sources of conflict or major sources of joy.

What is needed to make a marriage joyful and alive is to learn to
celebrate your differences. That means you can look at one another
and say, "It's all right for you to be you and for me to be me." Are
you at that place yet? If not, there's hope. When you understand and
learn how to implement the differences you each bring to the marriage, your satisfaction and love level will climb.

29 Simplifying Your Life

Is your life fairly simple or is it overloaded? Does someone own you? Do you think that last question a bit strange? It's not really. Too many people feel their lives are dictated by others—work demands, children, social commitments. Do you ever feel overwhelmed—like you're being stretched to a breaking point?

❖ How does stress and busyness impact your marriage?

❖ If your life was more balanced, how would you feel?

❖ What does a "fulfilled life" mean to you?

❖ If you were to have the life you really wanted, what would you need to do?

❖ What keeps you from changing your life?

❖ How would your spouse answer these questions?

30 Life and Busyness

What is your life like at this time? Is it disrupted and chaotic or is it harmonious and balanced? You may find your answer as you respond to and discuss the following questions.

❖ At the end of the day, do you feel frustrated and exhausted because you don't have very much to show for your efforts? How does this impact your marriage?

❖ Do you end up rushing to get things done on time at work and at home because of interruptions, crises, and unreasonable deadlines? How does this impact your marriage?

❖ Do you feel immobilized because of too many commitments? How does this impact your marriage?

❖ Do you run through your day at a fast rate, wishing you could go faster? How does this impact your marriage?

❖ Do you end up feeling guilty or angry because of what you haven't accomplished? How does this impact your marriage?

❖ What positive changes can you make at this time regarding busyness, and how can your spouse help you?

31 Superman Syndrome

Perhaps one of the most damaging beliefs we hold is that the best way to get something done is to do it ourselves. We're like the comic-based character Superman. He handled every problem by himself. Not once did he ask for help.

When I was younger, I thought there was only one Superman. But as I grew older, I began to discover many of his clones. Like Superman, these people never asked for help. How about you? Do you ask for help? Do you attempt to do everything and be all things to every person? If so, your life isn't fulfilling. In fact, it's super complicated. If you suffer from Superman or Superwoman Syndrome, you collect activities and are a master juggler. You're fueled by praise. "I don't know how you do so much." "You love to fly from one rescue operation to the next." You're everyone's helper, everyone's solution, the one who bails everyone out. You rarely take off your super cape. You end up being everyone's hero. So the big question is, how does this impact your marriage?

If you suspect you or your spouse suffers from Superman or Superwoman Syndrome, consider these questions:

- Do you rarely have any time just for you?
- Do you find it hard to say no to other people's needs?
- Are people constantly calling or asking you for something?
- Are you a problem solver for others?
- Is "delegation" a word that's foreign to you?
- Would you rather do things yourself or ask for help?
- Do you continue to improve on whatever you do?

❖ What do your answers say about your marriage? What changes, if any, need to be made?

32 Over-Involvement

What's your level of involvement in your church? Is it balanced? What's your level of involvement in the Christian life? Is it balanced? Are you serving Christ in some way? If so, who called you to this service?

Sometimes a pattern of over-involvement, clutter, and busyness that's part of our lives at home and at work might follow us into our spiritual lives unless we're vigilant. People often look to their church and their spiritual times as little oases of refreshment where they meet the living God who will help them make sense out of the chaos in their lives. Sadly, the oasis is frequently just another place of breathlessness and stress.

❖ Does your spiritual life refresh you or exhaust you?

❖ How is your marriage (attitude and behavior) different after you've concluded your times of devotions?

❖ How is your marriage (attitude and behavior) different after you've come home from a worship service?

❖ How is your marriage (attitude and behavior) different after you've finished teaching that Sunday school class or left that board meeting?

33 Listening

❖ What does "listening" mean to you? What is your definition?

❖ Describe in detail the times you feel your spouse really listens to you.

❖ On what topic would you like your spouse to listen to you more?

Consider what Scripture says about listening:

> He who gives an answer before he hears, it is folly and shame to him (Proverbs 18:13 NASB).

> Any story sounds true until someone tells the other side and sets the record straight (18:17 TLB).

> The wise man learns by listening; the simpleton can learn only by seeing scorners punished (21:11 TLB).

> Let every man be quick to hear [a ready listener] (James 1:19 AMP, brackets in original).

What is listening? Consider and discuss these points:

> Listening means that when your spouse is talking to you:

1. You are not thinking about what you are going to say when he/she stops talking. You are not busy formulating your response. You are concentrating on what is being said and are putting into practice Proverbs 18:13.

2. You are completely accepting what is being said without judging what he/she is saying or how he/she says it. You may fail to hear the message if you are thinking that you don't like your spouse's tone of voice or the words he/she is using. You may react on the spot to the tone and content and miss the meaning.

3. You should be able to repeat what your spouse has said and what you think he/she was feeling while speaking to you.

34   Encouragement

First Thessalonians 5:11 states, "Encourage one another and build each other up, just as in fact you are doing." You are like the refiner's fire. What you notice and encourage in others can be refined in a positive way. Any movement that you see headed in a healthy, positive direction needs your attention and reinforcement.[34] You're saying, "Go for it. You can do it!"

One character trait that enables a person to be an encourager is gentleness. This quality means that when you discover where another person is vulnerable or sensitive, you're not hard, harsh, or forceful with him or her. When you discover a tender, sensitive place in your spouse, you protect it rather than step on it. As you consider ways of encouraging your mate, ask yourself these questions:

- Am I gentle, especially with my partner's sensitive areas?
- Does my spouse feel safe around me even in those sensitive areas?
- Am I treating my spouse the way that I want to be treated?
- Am I building hope in his or her life?

❖ When was the last time your spouse thanked you for believing in him or her? What was the circumstance?

❖ If you had deposited a dollar in a bank account every time you complained to your spouse about his or her speech or actions, would you be able to pay for a new luxury car, a new wardrobe, or only a bag of groceries? What words or phrases, if banned from your speech, would stop putting cash into that bank account?

35 Reminders

Do you give reminders? If so, are they helpful or not? Reminders can actually cause the other person to rely on them to bail him or her out. Why would people use the energy to remember to do something when they have someone who will remind them? Have you ever made statements like these?

- "Honey, be sure you've got your wallet."
- "Don't forget to stop and pick up some milk and butter on the way home."
- "Don't you ever look at the gas gauge? You know how many times you've run out."
- "Be sure to take a coat with you. You usually get cold."
- "If I've asked you once, I've asked you a hundred times…"
- "You didn't call for the plane tickets. I'll do it for you…again."

❖ What reminders do you hear from your spouse?

❖ What reminders do you give to your spouse?

You may be thinking, *What's wrong with reminders? Aren't they just helpful remarks?* Perhaps they would be if you reminded your partner once or twice, and then he or she learned to remember on his or her own. Reminding once in a while may be helpful, but if you have to repeat reminders again and again, it's obvious they aren't working. They are becoming what I call bailout responses.

❖ What could you do instead of reminders that would work?

Which organ of the body is the most important for listening?

If you said your ears…try again. The answer is "eyes." Why do I say that? Every message has three components: (1) actual content, (2) tone of voice, and (3) nonverbal communication. It's possible to express many different messages using the same words, statements, or questions simply by changing your tone of voice or body movements. Nonverbal communication includes facial expression, body posture, and actions. The three components of communication must be complementary in their message for a concept to be transmitted clearly. Research suggests that successful communication consists primarily of nonverbal communication, followed by tone of voice, followed by actual content or words.

Tone is crucial. With your tone of voice you can also give a dozen different meanings to just one sentence. And your nonverbal cues can void your actual words. If you're trying to talk to one another from different rooms, you might be missing out on the nuances of the true message. You need to see the other person to get the entire communication. Don't talk until you can see the whites of their eyes.

❖ What tone of voice helps your communication?

❖ What tone of voice hinders it?

❖ Record one of your conversations some time and then listen to it together. You might be surprised at what you learn.

37   Gifts

Marriage is a gift. You may be the finest gift your spouse has ever received. Your spouse may be the finest gift you've ever received. A personal gift is usually an item that is selected with care and consideration. Its purpose is to bring delight and fulfillment to another person. Gifts can be an expression of deep feeling on the part of the giver. Think of the care and effort you put into selecting a gift for someone you care about. You feel excited and up for the challenge of selecting and presenting the perfect gift for your loved one.

You are a gift to your spouse. If you consider that you are a gift, how do you live so that your spouse feels that he or she has been given a special gift? Does your spouse experience delight, fulfillment, and a feeling of being special when spending time with you?

On the receiving end of the gift, how do you react when you receive a special gift that brings you delight? If your spouse is a special gift to you, how do you treat this gift? Does your partner feel as though he/she really is a gift to you?

A gift is given as an expression of love. It's not based on whether the recipient deserves it or not. Giving a gift is actually an act of grace.

❖ What is the best tangible gift your spouse has ever given you?

❖ What is the best tangible gift you've ever given your spouse?

❖ What is the best intangible gift your spouse has ever given you?

❖ What is the best intangible gift you've ever given to your spouse?

❖ What gift would you like to give to your spouse?

❖ What would your spouse most appreciate?

38   Being Kind and Compassionate

If you had to base your marriage on one Bible verse, what would it be? How about Ephesians 4:32? "Be kind and compassionate to one another, forgiving each other, just as in Christ God forgave you."

❖ What would your marriage be like if it were based on this verse? Write out three ideas and then share and discuss them.

In line with Ephesians 4:32, consider these two suggestions regarding debts and kindness.

Cancel debts. Forgiving other people just as God in Christ has forgiven you means *canceling* the debts. It also means resisting the impulse to bring them up again because they're now in the past. This may mean asking your spouse to forgive you if you bring up old problems in the heat of an argument.

❖ Identify a personal debt in your marriage relationship you would like canceled at this time in your life.

Be kind. Webster's dictionary defines "kindness" as "being sympathetic, gentle and benevolent." Forgiveness springs much easier from an attitude of kindness than from an attitude of defensiveness.

❖ How would you like your spouse to be even gentler than he or she is at this time in your marriage?

39   Intimacy

Strong marriages are built on intimacy. Think of marriage like a house. Those built based on human love and human intimacy are like two of the houses in the "Three Little Pigs" story. In time, the huffs and puffs of pressures and problems will blow them down. If you want a lasting, enjoyable marriage, build it on a solid foundation of spiritual intimacy, which has the strength of concrete and steel.

❖   If you had to define spiritual intimacy for someone else, how would you describe it?

❖   Discuss what obstacles you need to overcome to strengthen your marriage's level of spiritual intimacy.

40   What Is Marriage?

❖ If you had to speak to a group and share your definition of marriage, describe what you would say and then share your definition with your spouse.

Now, read these quotes together and share your thoughts.

- "Marriage is a covenant of responsible love, a fellowship of repentance and forgiveness."[1]
- "Marriage is a total commitment of the *total* person for the *total* life."[2]
- "Marriage does not demand perfection. But it must be given priority. It is an institution for sinners. No one else need apply. But it finds its finest glory when sinners see it as God's way of leading us through His ultimate curriculum of love and righteousness."[3]

41   Romance

❖ How do you define "romance"?

❖ How does your spouse define "romance"?

❖ What is romantic about your daily life together?

❖ What actions on your part create romance for you?

❖ What actions on your spouse's part create romance for you?

❖ Describe a romantic getaway you would like to experience with your spouse. Where would it be? What would you do? How would it be different from your daily life? What would you wear? Where would you eat? What would be the décor, music, fragrances, conversation topics, and so forth?

❖ What would it take for that romantic getaway to actually happen?

❖ How can you create a home version of your "romantic getaway"?

42   Sex Is a Process

Sex is about the *process* of enjoying pleasure, not about your spouse pleasing you or you pleasing your spouse. "Mutual pleasure" is the refrain of sexual fulfillment. Ultimately, your spouse will be pleased only when you are pleased, and you will be pleased only when you respond to your natural instincts of extending and enjoying pleasure.

Sexual expertise is learned. A good goal is for the two of you to become authorities on yourselves and freely communicate your awareness of your likes and dislikes to each other. Become sex experts about each other. Your spouse won't know your sexual hungers and desires unless you tell him or her, and vice versa. Because preferences change from time to time, telling your spouse once is not enough.[4]

❖ How do you know when your spouse wants more out of sex than just sex?

❖ What does "intimacy" mean to you?

❖ What does "intimacy" mean to your spouse?

❖ How do you blend your two views so both of you get your intimacy needs met?

❖ What are some of the most romantic things you've ever done for your spouse?

❖ Describe how they affected your relationship in other areas.

❖ How does your physical relationship with your spouse promote wholeness in the emotional, mental, and spiritual aspects of your life?

43 Conflicts

❖ What are the three most positive memories you have of your spouse over the past five years? Share why these are important to you.

Now consider this thought:

> Often the thoughts we have about our spouses are negative. We rehearse in our minds what they've done wrong or what they haven't done. We rehearse their failures. Scripture doesn't say to do this.

Is that an interesting and new concept for you—"rehearsing failure"? Many of us live on that stage, constantly mulling over our spouses' failures that we remember. Instead, I believe we should be focusing on the instances where God worked in their lives and how He will continue to work in their lives now and in the future.

If you find this rehearsal of positive memories awkward or difficult, start with small steps. Make a list of your spouse's positive qualities—the things he or she does to build up your life together. Memorize this list and contemplate how much harder life would be without your spouse and his or her positive qualities.

Often when I talk with couples about their conflicts, their attention is on what creates conflict. Who started it may not be as important as how and why it ends. This concept is called a "truce trigger." It's when you shift your attention to the conflict-ending events rather than the beginning events. The shift may help you discover why and how the conflict started.

❖ Where do your conflicts usually occur?

❖ When do your conflicts usually occur?

❖ Describe how your conflicts usually end.

44   Your Worth

How much is your partner worth? How much are you worth? Your partner and you have inestimable value to God and to each other. That's fact. But are you *really* aware of your worth? Do you really believe that you have value?

❖ What does your partner do or say that lets you know he or she highly values you?

❖ How do you communicate your spouse's value to him or her?

Jesus told a story about a pearl to communicate the value He places on you. "The kingdom of heaven is like a merchant looking for fine pearls. When he found one of great value, he went away and sold everything he had and bought it" (Matthew 13:45-46). Jesus went into the slave market of sin and paid for your release. Paul wrote that "you were bought at a price" (1 Corinthians 6:20). Now take a moment to read 1 Peter 1:18-19:

> You know that it was not with perishable things such as silver or gold that you were redeemed from the empty way of life handed down to you from your ancestors, but with the precious blood of Christ, a lamb without blemish or defect.

God paid a great price for you!

We usually give preferential treatment to the items of great value we possess. If you had a painting by a struggling amateur artist on your wall, you probably wouldn't install a burglar alarm to protect it or worry that it would be stolen when you went out. It's not that valuable. But if you owned a Van Gogh or Monet, you probably wouldn't feel safe keeping it at home at all. Paintings by those masters are so valuable that they usually end up in carefully guarded private collections or museums. The value of an item usually determines the way we treat it.

Since God places such high value on you, you deserve to be treated with respect, care, and love. But wait! Before you admonish your partner to treat you with more respect, think about these questions.

❖ Do you treat yourself with respect, care, and love? Give specific examples.

❖ Do you treat your partner with respect, care, and love? Give specific examples.

45 Worship

"What did you get out of the last worship service you attended?" Have you ever asked your partner that question? It's interesting, isn't it? It assumes that people go to worship services to get something out of them. But is that the true purpose of worship? "Worship" means "reverence to God." It means acknowledging God for who He is. It means recognizing Him. The focus of worship is supposed to be on God, not us.

Think for a moment about the significant times in your spiritual life.

❖ When did you experience significant moments of worship in which you knew you encountered God? Have you shared them with your partner? Would he or she be able to describe them to another person?

❖ Talk about worship in your personal and marital life.

❖ How can you help your partner worship more?

❖ Share your concept of God with each other.

Yes, these may be new thoughts for both of you. Focusing on God will enrich your lives and your marriage.

If anyone can control his tongue, it proves that he has perfect control over himself in every other way (James 3:2 TLB).

Anyone who says he is a Christian but doesn't control his sharp tongue is just fooling himself, and his religion isn't worth much (1:26 TLB).

Let him who wants to enjoy life and see good days [good—whether apparent or not] keep his tongue free from evil and his lips from guile (treachery, deceit) (1 Peter 3:10 AMP, brackets in original).

Death and life are in the power of the tongue, and they who indulge in it shall eat the fruit of it [for death or life] (Proverbs 18:21 AMP, brackets in original).

These verses contain strong words, but they are true.

❖ What do these Scriptures mean for your marriage?

❖ How can they help you improve your relationship?

47   Temptation

Do you find it easy to say, "I'm wrong," "I did it," or "I'm responsible"? Probably not—especially to your partner. We seem to follow Adam's pattern of blaming. He blamed Eve and then blamed God for giving him Eve (Genesis 3:12). Within each of us is a tendency to respond to life with our old nature. This is commonly referred to as the "sin nature." It's in *every* person. And sometimes we not only give in to it, we actually nourish it and give it life and power. The responsibility for our sinful thoughts and responses is ours alone. We have to shoulder that load. Giving in to that old nature is a *choice* we make. We don't have to!

> No temptation has overtaken you except what is common to mankind. And God is faithful; he will not let you be tempted beyond what you can bear. But when you are tempted, he will also provide a way out so that you can endure it (1 Corinthians 10:13).

❖ What temptation does your partner struggle with the most?

❖ How can you help him or her resist it?

❖ What is the greatest struggle with temptation in your marriage?

❖ How can that struggle be overcome?

48 Vows

Imagine for a moment that your wedding to your partner is taking place today. If you were to rewrite your wedding vows now, what would you commit to and promise to do? Before you think of your own answers, consider what other couples have written:

> "I realize that our love will change. I will work to maintain a high level of romance, courtship, and love in our relationship."

> "I pledge myself to confront problems when they arise and not retreat like a turtle into my shell."

> "I will respect your beliefs and capabilities, which are different from mine, and I will not attempt to make you into a revised edition of me."

> "I will reflect the Word of God in my relationship with you."

❖ Which of these would you select for your marriage? Explain.

❖ Take a few moments to write out new marriage vows.

Many couples write out vows each year as they celebrate their wedding anniversary. It adds a new dimension to the commitment of marriage.

49   Spiritual Growth

"Lay aside the old self... [and] be renewed in the spirit of your mind, and put on the new self" (Ephesians 4:22,24 NASB). Christian growth is a daily process of taking off attitudes, beliefs, and behaviors that reflect our old lifestyles before we accepted Christ and putting on those that reflect the presence of Christ in our lives. This Ephesians passage teaches that the only way any of us can progressively succeed in this daily process is by being renewed in the spirit of our mind. The renewal described is basically an act of God's Spirit powerfully influencing our spirit, attitude, state of mind, and disposition with respect to God and spiritual truths.

❖ What thoughts do you or your partner struggle with that reflect more of the old self than the new self?

❖ Have you ever shared and prayed about these together?

One of the joys of marriage is sharing your spiritual struggles and encouraging each other.

❖ Where are you today in your spiritual understanding compared to where you were one or two years ago?

❖ What are your plans for growing together spiritually this year?

50   Wedding Day

Find your wedding album and take out a photograph of your entire wedding party. As you sit and look at the photo (if no photo is available, recall by name the people who were in your wedding party), reflect back on that special day. Can you remember...

- What your mother and father said to you that day?
- What the minister said to you before the ceremony?
- How the minister prayed for you during the ceremony?
- What the people in your wedding party meant to you?

❖ Would you have the minister pray the same prayer for your marriage today?

❖ Where are the people in your wedding party today, and how are they doing?

❖ If you got married today, what would you do differently during the next six months than you did during the first six months?

❖ In what way would Jesus Christ's place in your marriage be different today than when you got married?

Take time today to reflect, share your memories, and give thanks to God for your marriage.

There are two major problems that can occur in any marriage. Well, more than that, but right now let's consider these: criticism and silence.

❖ When you hear criticism directed toward you, how do you interpret it?

❖ What does criticism mean to you?

❖ How does criticism make you feel?

❖ When your spouse is silent and won't talk to you, what does that mean to you?

Think about this: Most men hear criticism as contempt and often withdraw into silence, which many women interpret as hostility. The more a husband is silent, the more his wife becomes angry. Think about that in respect to how your spouse and you respond. Is there an answer? Yes![5]

Together, read aloud these verses from the book of Proverbs:

> Sin is not ended by multiplying words, but the prudent hold their tongues (10:19).

> Whoever would foster love covers over an offense, but whoever repeats the matter separates close friends (17:9).

> Gracious words are a honeycomb, sweet to the soul and healing to the bones (16:24).

> Whoever heeds life-giving correction will be at home

among the wise. Those who disregard discipline despise themselves, but the one who heeds correction gains understanding (15:31-32).

❖ Will these verses impact or change the way you relate to each other when it comes to criticism?

52 Create an Anniversary Card

When is your anniversary? Today I invite you to take the opportunity to be a writer and create your own anniversary card (even if it isn't your anniversary). This is your opportunity to open your heart and pour forth the benefits and blessings of your marriage. Be as creative, and bold, and descriptive as you can.

Plan a special time to get together and share your cards.

❖ How did this interactive opportunity influence your relationship?

❖ Some couples celebrate their anniversary monthly. Will you consider celebrating yours more often than you currently do?

53 Are You Cherished?

❖ How does your spouse make you feel unique and special?

❖ What would you like your spouse to do to help you feel special?

❖ What can you do to help your spouse feel more cherished?

After discussing those questions, talk about how these passages of Scripture would apply.

> Be kind and compassionate to one another, forgiving each other, just as in Christ God forgave you (Ephesians 4:32).

> Rejoice with those who rejoice; mourn with those who mourn (Romans 12:15).

54   Common Phrases in Your Marriage

We all have phrases spoken to us that impact us as individuals as well as marriage partners. Have you considered the comments your spouse and you exchange frequently?

❖ What five phrases do you not like to hear from your spouse?

❖ What five phrases do you like to hear from your spouse?

❖ What five phrases do you think your spouse would rather not hear from you?

❖ What five phrases would your spouse like to hear from you more often?

❖ What can you do about the phrases you don't like to hear?

Talk about how these passages from the book of Proverbs can help your communication with each other.

> Everyone enjoys giving good advice, and how wonderful it is to be able to say the right thing at the right time! (15:23 TLB).

> Timely advice is as lovely as gold apples in a silver basket (25:11 TLB).

> A friendly discussion is as stimulating as the sparks that fly when iron strikes iron (27:17 TLB).

55   Scolding

❖ Define what the word "scold" means to you.

Now think back to when you were a child and resurrect times when your parents scolded you.

❖ What do you remember them saying?

❖ What was their tone of voice?

❖ How did you feel?

❖ How did you respond?

❖ Does scolding occur in your marriage? If yes, do you react the same way you did as a child?

When a spouse "scolds," he or she is trying to correct something. But when people are scolded, they feel like someone is looking down on them, judging them. They often feel like children in trouble.

❖ Do you tend to scold?

Read through the book of Proverbs, especially chapter 15, and write down five verses that you can use to guide you in helping or correcting another person.

❖ Why not memorize those five verses as a good reminder to keep your speech gentle and encouraging?

56   Marrying Someone Like You?

What if your son or daughter grew up and married someone just like you? Think about this for a moment.

❖ What are the reasons you think this would be a good idea?

❖ What are the reasons you think it might not be such a good idea?

❖ What do your answers say about how you respond to your spouse in your marriage?

❖ Describe the person you would like your son or daughter to marry.

❖ Which passage of Scripture would you like to see lived out in their married life?

57   Closeness

❖ What three things do you do that cause your spouse to be more open toward you and want to stay close?

Now consider and discuss how you do in these areas:

- You listen and can repeat back what was said.
- You say, "I appreciate your sharing that with me."
- You don't interrupt.
- You see something that needs to be done, and you do it without a lot of hassle.
- You share your feelings.
- You say, "Let's talk."
- Your face shows you want to talk.
- You pray with your spouse.
- You give your mate your full attention—no grunting response.[6]

❖ Write down three statements you tend to make that *don't work* when your needs aren't being met.

Here are some suggestions from Dr. Emerson Eggerichs that may work. Discuss what you think about them and whether they would help in your situation.

- "When you said you didn't want to spend time talking about my concerns, that felt unloving to me."

- "When you gave me a quick solution to what I was trying to tell you, that felt unloving."

- "When you make negative remarks about my work goals, that feels disrespectful."

- "When you suggest that I am irresponsible, that feels disrespectful."

- "When you roll your eyes and say, 'That's ridiculous,' that doesn't work."

- "When you said you were just too tired to have sex, that felt like rejection. I understand that you're tired, but I hope you understand my need as well. It's not that I'm just oversexed; I really need to hold you close."[7]

❖ Brainstorm with your spouse positive ways both of you can communicate when your needs aren't being met.

59   What Would You Like to Hear?

❖ What are the three best statements you've learned to make in your marriage?

Here are some positive communication suggestions I've compiled from my years of counseling and helping others.

- "I'd like to talk for 15 minutes when it's comfortable for you."
- "Are you looking for a solution or just a listening ear?"
- "I have an extra 20 minutes tonight. How would you like me to use it?"
- "I'm interested in your input and suggestions on this subject."
- "How would you like me to pray for you today?"
- "I appreciate what you did for me tonight. Thank you."
- "You know what? You were right, and I was wrong."
- "I don't know all you do around here, but I know it's a lot."

❖ What three statements would you like to hear more often?

Dr. Gary and Barbara Rosberg talk about six loves that have their basis in Scripture:

> *Forgiving love offers a fresh start after you have offended and hurt each other.* Forgiving love equips you to communicate such a deep level of acceptance for each other that you can recover from the pain you occasionally inflict on each other and work through your offenses.

> *Serving love helps you discover and meet each other's deepest needs.* Serving to meet [the deepest needs] in each other.

> *Persevering love sustains you through the trials of life.* You need to love in ways that keep your marriage firmly grounded through the stormy trials and pains of life.

> *Guarding love protects your hearts from threats to your marriage.* If you are not aware of the threats to your marriage or the potential havoc these forces can wreak on your relationship, then you are vulnerable.

> *Celebrating love equips you to maintain a satisfying emotional, physical, and spiritual connection.* Celebrating love keeps the spark alive, not only in the bedroom but also in all areas of the relationship.

> *Renewing love regards the marriage covenant as unbreakable.*

These six loves are the secret to lasting love. As you begin to practice loving in the ways that God instructs, you will shield your marriage from the ravages of disappointment, discouragement, distance, disconnect, discord, and emotional divorce.[8]

❖ Which of these six loves do each of you need to strengthen? How will you accomplish this?

61 Who Do You Put First?

Are you a list maker? Many people are. Even if you're not into making lists, you probably have a priority list in your mind. Who or what is usually at the top? For many people, they are at the top of their own lists. They want their own needs met first. Or it could be that work is their first priority. God has a better idea! Put Him first, and then your spouse, and then sort through the rest.

❖ In what ways do you feel you're at the top of your spouse's list (after God, of course)?

❖ In what ways is your spouse at the top of your list?

❖ Do you need to make your mate a bigger priority? If so, how will you do that?

❖ What steps can you take to make sure God is at the top of your priority list?

62   Failures and Forgiveness

There are times of failure in all marriages. Many couples live with regrets of what they did or didn't do. Some have a storehouse of failures, while others have a few. Some people prefer to bury these, and some bring them up repeatedly. Neither way works. Burying issues keeps them going because they're still alive, and constant reminders of failure create distance in relationships.

❖ What failures have each of you experienced in your marriage?

❖ What have you done with them? Was it effective?

Relationship author Gary Chapman suggests identifying failures, confessing them, repenting of them, and then applying forgiveness. He suggests three benefits:

- You will no longer fear the past because you have confessed your failures and have been forgiven.

- Your marriage relationship will be deepened when you and your spouse experience genuine confession, repentance, and forgiveness. Forgiveness makes possible the restoration of your marriage relationship.

- In forgiving others, you become more like Christ. In other words, dealing with past failures is a huge step toward spiritual maturity.[9]

❖ What's your next step regarding failures in your marriage?

* ❖ Describe what you believe "spiritual intimacy" means.

* ❖ How do you see it existing in your marriage?

Gary and Barbara Rosberg discuss spiritual intimacy in their book *6 Secrets to a Lasting Love*:

> What is spiritual intimacy? There is nothing weird or mystical about it. Spiritual intimacy occurs when you as husband and wife surrender your lives and relationship to the Lord. You grow together spiritually when you live out your marriage relationship according to God's ways and aim to please him in all things.
>
> You may not realize the power of spiritual intimacy in…celebrating love in your relationship.
>
> *Spiritual intimacy empowers celebrating love.*
>
> *Spiritual intimacy allows you to connect at the deepest level.* If you want the deepest possible connection with your spouse, this is it.
>
> *Spiritual intimacy links you with God's purposes and plans for you.*
>
> *Spiritual intimacy allows you to bless each other with God's love.* As husbands or wives, you can demonstrate what God's love for your spouse looks like. You can be God's voice and arms of love and care.
>
> *Spiritual intimacy brings your deepest values and desires into agreement.* As you and your spouse

grow spiritually intimate and submit to the teachings of Scripture, your biggest goals and beliefs will be in harmony.

Spiritual intimacy opens the door to the deepest levels of communication. Spiritual intimacy permits profound sharing you cannot enjoy at any other level.

Spiritual intimacy empowers your marriage to survive.

Spiritual intimacy connects you to a supportive body of fellow disciples. No marriage survives or thrives by itself. God has given you his people, the church, to stand with you when you struggle and celebrate with you when you triumph.[10]

64 Who Makes the Decisions?

Let's consider decision-making. Which of you makes decisions more quickly? What effect does this have? In any relationship it is normal for one person to be quicker and more decisive. The quicker spouse inserts his or her thoughts, plans, and procedures into the discussion first and has a strong influence. He or she has the advantage; thus, the slower person tends to become even slower and can't keep pace.

It is better to have a commitment between both spouses to get involved in the overall decision-making process. You need to develop a "couple pace" for making decisions rather than maintain your individual paces. The slow person can learn to go a bit faster, and the faster one can learn to slow down. The point is to formulate your decisions together. "[It is] essential to realize that the spouse who *makes* the decisions is *not* necessarily the spouse who *controls* them. The key question ultimately is, '*Who decides* who decides?'"[11]

Here are some important questions to consider.

❖ Do you have difficulty making decisions? Does your spouse?

❖ Is the responsibility for making specific decisions based on your abilities and giftedness?

❖ Does one spouse fail to assume responsibility for making decisions, thus forcing the other to make the decisions?

❖ Why is it important to discuss your methods for making decisions?

❖ Is the plan your spouse and you have in place for decision-making successful?

❖ Have you agreed to make decisions in certain areas on your own without input from your spouse?

❖ What are some of the major decisions each of you make?

❖ Do your thoughts and decisions reflect your relationship with the Lord?

65   Your Family Tree

When we marry, we all bring along emotional baggage. Some of this comes from our family of origin, especially our parents. Yes, they influence our marriages. Even as adults we sometimes still hear their voices in our heads. You learned a lot about marriage from them, and it's important to be aware of their impact on your view of marriage.

❖ On a scale of 1 to 10, rate your perception of the happiness of your parents' marriage (1 being very unhappy and 10 being very happy).

❖ What did you learn about marriage from your mother?

❖ What did you learn about marriage from your father?

❖ How is each parent influencing your marriage today, directly and indirectly?

❖ In what way is your spouse most similar to your opposite-sex parent?

❖ What unresolved or unfinished issues remain between you and your mother and/or father?

66 Your Parents and You

Let's consider in more detail your mother and father's influence on your life and your marriage. Your spouse may have some insights that are different than yours, so listen carefully to his or her opinions too.

❖ Describe how you feel about each parent.

❖ Describe how you think each parent feels about you.

❖ What emotions does each parent express openly? How do they express them?

❖ List the positive qualities of your father. Which of these have become part of your life?

❖ List the negative qualities of your father. Which of these have become part of your life?

❖ How do the qualities listed in the previous two questions impact your marriage?

❖ List the positive qualities of your mother. Which of these have become part of your life?

❖ List the negative qualities of your mother. Which of these have become part of your life?

❖ How do the qualities in the last two questions impact your marriage?

❖ Describe your most unpleasant and pleasant experiences with each parent.

67 Children

Children always impact your marriage no matter their ages or whether you have one or ten. When children arrive your lives change.

To what extent are children the source of problems or tension between you and your spouse?

Often   Sometimes   Rarely   Never

To what extent are stepchildren the source of problems or tension between you and your spouse?

Often   Sometimes   Rarely   Never

We have differences and/or conflicts over...

_____ amount of time with children

_____ chores

_____ discipline

_____ favoritism

_____ other (please describe):

To what extent are in-laws the source of problems or tension between your spouse and you when it comes to your children?

Often   Sometimes   Rarely   Never

❖ What are the steps you can take to resolve any of these issues and create a more positive relationship with your partner?

68   Loss

Loss is a normal part of our lives on earth. With each and every one comes the potential for change, growth, insights, better understanding, and character refinement—all positive descriptions and words of hope. But these positives usually come in the future. In the midst of pain, it's often difficult to see that far ahead.

❖ Reflect on one of the earliest significant losses in your life. What happened? When did it occur? How old were you? Where was it? Who were the people involved?

❖ How did you react to the loss?

❖ Did anyone advise you on how to deal effectively with the loss?

❖ What did you learn then that may be hindering the way you cope with loss today?

❖ What did you learn about loss at an early age that helps you today?

❖ How have your early losses impacted your marriage?

69   What Bothers You?

❖ If something really bothers you about your spouse, how do you usually express it?

❖ Is there a better way to handle it? Explain.

❖ How would your spouse want you to express your feelings?

❖ If something about you really bothered your spouse, how would he or she express it?

❖ How would you want your spouse to express his or her feelings to you?

The way we express our concerns to one another is important. Delivery can be everything. If we feel attacked, we'll probably be defensive. Some people tend to bottle up their feelings and concerns, but then they accumulate until there is a blowup. The book of Proverbs gives us some wise guidance on handling sticky situations.

> A man who refuses to admit his mistakes can never be successful. But if he confesses and forsakes them, he gets another chance (28:13 TLB).

> Timely advice is as lovely as gold apples in a silver basket (25:11 TLB).

> Those who guard their mouths and their tongues keep themselves from calamity (21:23).

❖ Explore how these verses will help your spouse and you express your concerns in ways the other person can hear and accept.

70   Anger

❖ What makes you angry? In other words, when you're
   angered, what is usually occurring?

Basically, all of your answers can be placed into one of three cat-
egories. Anger is the result of (1) frustration, (2) hurt, or (3) fear.
Anger is not the first thing that you feel. *Anger is a secondary emotion*,
which means it is *always* preceded by one of those three primary
emotions. Becoming frustrated, hurt, or fearful (primary emotions)
frequently leads to feelings of anger. Unmet expectations, having to
make adjustments, problematic interferences—all of these situations can cause frustration that, in turn, can lead to anger.

Being the recipient of personal rejection, thoughtless words, care-
less deeds…any of these incidents can cause a mate to feel deeply
hurt. With the pain comes anger. Fear, regardless of the precipitant,
will lead to anger.[1]

Anger serves a very useful purpose. It functions as a motivator. Through personal discomfort, anger informs us that there are things we do not like—things that may need correcting. It then gives us the impetus to deal with them. Through anger, we are energized to act. It implores us to do things better, whether the "better" be with relationships or situations. At least this is its positive and healthy potential. Granted, we do not need anger in its aggressiveness. But we do need anger.[2]

❖ Ask each other, "When I'm angry, what is the best way for me to express it to you?"

❖ Read the following verses and discuss how you can put them into practice in your marriage.

> "In your anger do not sin": Do not let the sun go down while you are still angry (Ephesians 4:26).

> He who is slow to anger is better than the mighty, he who rules his [own] spirit than he who takes a city (Proverbs 16:32 AMP, brackets in original).

> Good sense makes a man restrain his anger, and it is his glory to overlook a transgression or an offense (Proverbs 19:11 AMP).

72   Intimacy Needs
Part 1

In this reading and the next two, we're going to look at the top 10 intimacy needs in marriage. When these needs are met, both of you usually realize satisfaction. First consider these three:

1. *Attention.* Attention means thinking about the other person, focusing on him or her by listening with your eyes and your ears in addition to showing interest, concern, and support. It's a bit like entering into the other person's world.

2. *Acceptance.* The best description I've heard of the quality of acceptance in love is more than 30 years old: "Acceptance is an unconditional commitment to an imperfect person."

3. *Appreciation and praise.* Each person needs appreciation and praise. Appreciation is gratefulness that is verbalized.

❖ In what ways would your spouse like you to give him or her more attention?

❖ How can you meet that need?

❖ In what ways would your spouse like you to accept him or her unconditionally?

❖ How can you meet this need?

❖ In what ways would your spouse like you to show more appreciation and offer more praise?

❖ How can you meet this need?

❖ Make a list of every helpful or positive thing you can remember that your spouse does or has done. Then set aside a time to share your appreciation for each other.

73 Intimacy Needs
Part 2

Let's consider the next four top intimacy needs in marriage.

1. *Encouragement.* Believing in your spouse.

2. *Support.* The need for support in intimacy is described in the Bible as bearing one another's burdens. This doesn't mean doing what you think is best. It means discovering exactly how your spouse would like to be supported.

3. *Affection.* Affection is a basic ingredient of marriage. It can mean anything from a sexual interchange to a nonsexual touch. Affectionate touching generates the sensations of warmth, security, and emotional satisfaction craved by every human being.

4. *Approval.* Approval is giving positive affirmation and thinking and speaking well of someone. It can be expressed in a word or a look.

❖ In what ways would your spouse like to be encouraged by you?

❖ How can you encourage your spouse more?

❖ In what ways would your spouse like you to show more support? Will you do this?

❖ In what ways would your spouse like you to show more affection? Are you willing to do this?

❖ In what ways would your spouse like you to show more approval? Are you going to do this?

74 Intimacy Needs
Part 3

Consider the last three intimacy needs in marriage:

1. *Security.* This involves trust. It means you can depend on the one in whom you trust. You can rely on that person's word. You can count on that person to back you up and praise you, not only in your presence but also when you're not around.

2. *Comfort and empathy.* Having someone who understands you, identifies with you, and can, therefore, comfort you is an important need. It is also an admonition from Scripture: "Encourage one another daily" (Hebrews 3:13). Comfort consoles in a way that touches the heart of the other person.

3. *Respect.* Although both men and women need respect, men seem to need it more. When you respect people, you value them. You have a high regard for them and you honor them. At the top of any man's list of needs is receiving respect from his mate; God created men that way. A man needs respect as much as he needs air to breathe.

❖ How can you show your spouse that he or she is secure with you?

❖ How can you give your spouse more comfort and empathy?

❖ How can you show your spouse that you respect him or her? How often will you do this?

75 Budgets

Budgets help couples more than they hurt—honest. In fact, they have saved some couples from disaster.

> When budgets are created to benefit one spouse at the expense of the other or when money is spent by one spouse without considering the feelings of the other, it diminishes love. It's that simple. But when financial planning considers the feelings of both spouses, it's a wise financial plan that also builds romantic love.[3]
>
> A budget helps you discover what a certain quality of life really costs. To more fully understand the quality of life you can afford consider three budgets. One that describes what you *need*, one that describes what you *want*, and one that describes what you can *afford*.
>
> - The *needs budget* should include the monthly cost of meeting the necessities of your life, items you would be uncomfortable without.
>
> - The *wants budget* includes the cost of meeting all your needs and wants—things that bring special pleasure to your life.
>
> - The *affordable budget* begins with your income and should first include the cost of meeting your most important needs.[4]

❖ On a scale of 1 (very insecure) to 5 (very secure), how secure do you feel with the financial support you have in your marriage?[5]

❖ Have you thought much about your total income and how

it affects your standard of living? If so, how do you feel about it?[6]

❖ Are you willing to reduce your standard of living so that you can live within your income?[7]

You talk to yourself. Yep, it's true. We all do. And that's normal. And what we say to ourselves often determines what we do, how we respond, and what we're feeling. When what we say is tied into our frustration and anger, we generally aren't gentle with ourselves.

❖ What are three frequent statements you say to yourself when you're upset?

Your inner conversation—also called self-talk—is where frustrations are either tamed or inflamed. How you behave and what you say to others is influenced by how you talk to yourself about their behaviors and responses too. Changing your inner conversation to a more positive tone is essential in keeping frustrations from erupting into wounding words and actions.

There will be times when you know in advance that you'll encounter a situation that may lead to someone—you—getting angry. If you listen carefully to what you usually say in similar situations, you may identify two important things: what is generating your anger and what you can do to adjust your attitude. You may also discover how you can alter your expectations so that type of situation will be less anger producing. Here are some examples of anger-reducing self-talk:

- "I won't take what is said or done personally."
- "No matter what happens, I know I can control my frustrations and anger. I have this capability because of the presence of Jesus in my life."
- "I'm going to stay calm and in control."
- "I will respond to statements that usually trigger my

anger by saying, 'That's interesting,' 'I'll think about that,' or 'Will you tell me more about this situation?'"

- "I don't have to allow this situation to bother me."
- "If I begin to get upset, I will take some deep breaths, slow down my thoughts, delay my responses, and purposely speak in a soft tone."

God's Word has a lot to say about how we think. If you have difficulty with negative inner conversations, I suggest writing out the following Scriptures on index cards. Read them aloud every morning and evening.

Isaiah 26:3

Romans 8:6-7

2 Corinthians 10:5

Ephesians 4:22-24

Philippians 4:6-9

1 Peter 1:13-16

77   Decisions

❖ Reflecting on the past year, what are six major decisions that were made by your spouse, you, or both of you?

❖ Go back over that now and indicate how each decision was made or arrived at.

❖ What is the typical style of decision-making in your marriage?

❖ How do you feel about this approach? Can it be improved?

Healthy couples make time for having fun and relaxing together. Before marriage, this dynamic is quite natural for most couples. In fact, that's how people fall in love with each other. Read and follow the suggestions Ron Deal and David Olson share in their book *The Remarriage Checkup*:

> Time. We have all the time in the world and yet finding time—or is it making time?—to sustain and grow your marriage can be difficult...
>
> Strong [couples] have an active, shared leisure life. When the definitions of fun differ, couples...seek a balance between giving each other the freedom to pursue individual interests and making sacrifices so they can spend time together. Other couples just naturally share the same idea of what's fun, and they pursue it on a regular basis...
>
> 1. Brainstorm a list of the leisure activities you enjoy together. Be sure to mention "biggies" (e.g., a seven-day cruise) and "little ones" (e.g., playing cards after dinner). A healthy marriage has some of both.
>
>   • Now discuss which ones are easiest to implement at this stage of your life.
>
>   • Which ones have gotten lost in the family forest but you'd like to rediscover them?
>
> 2. List the leisure activities you don't enjoy doing together. It's okay to have an individual interest or activity that you enjoy as long as investing

in it doesn't steal time from the marriage. Learning to appreciate your partner's interests is also respectful. [8]

How is your relational bank account? Clifford Notarius and Howard Markman explain this concept in their book *We Can Work It Out*:

> One of the metaphors used to describe a couple's interaction is that of a bank account. There are variations of this, but one is called a Relationship Bank Account.
>
> As is true of any bank account, the balance in the Relational Bank is in flux because of deposits and withdrawals. Relationship deposits vary in size just like our monetary deposits. They could be a kind of work or action or a very large gift of love. Withdrawals also vary. A minor disagreement could be small, but a major offense could drain the account.
>
> When you begin thinking of your relationship in this way, you can be more aware of deposits and attempted deposits as well as what constitutes a withdrawal. Naturally the larger the balance the healthier the relationship.
>
> If there is a large balance in the account, a few small withdrawals don't impact the account that much. But if the balance is relatively small or hovers around zero, a small withdrawal is definitely felt. The ideal is to keep the deposits high and the withdrawals low.
>
> If you will increase your positive actions toward each other, these will eventually crowd out and eliminate the negative. The consequences of behaving in a positive way override the negative.[9]

❖ How do you and your spouse make deposits into your marriage account?

❖ What constitutes withdrawals for both of you?

❖ Discuss the balance in your marriage account and what you can do to add more to it.

Sometimes our behaviors and habits irritate people. You know what I mean. When people do that, they're often referred to as being a pain in the neck. And some behaviors and habits are actually destructive.

❖ Name one or two habits or behaviors you do that some might consider annoying.

Consider what Dr. Willard Harley says: "A destructive act (one occurrence) is bad enough. But a destructive marital habit is repeated over and over. It is particularly important to overcome it because it multiplies the damage of single acts."[10] So what do we do to try to get rid of what we don't like in another person? Do we make a request? Probably not. No, we tend to demand.

> Demands serve a short-sighted purpose. They're used by a spouse to force a mate to care when the mate is unwilling.

> So, what can you do? Here are some suggestions:

>> *Step 1:* Explain what you would like and ask how your spouse would feel fulfilling your request. This first step makes all the difference in the world. You have turned what would have been a selfish demand into a thoughtful request by simply asking how your spouse would feel about it.

>> *Step 2:* If your spouse indicates that the request will be unpleasant to fulfill, withdraw the request.

>> *Step 3:* Discuss alternative ways your spouse could help you and feel good about it. If your

marriage is healthy, your spouse probably wants to help you or meet your needs even when turning down your request. It's the way you want your spouse to help that often causes the problem. Unless you present your request thoughtfully, you will not get what you want for the long term.

Thoughtfulness is constructive. Selfishness is destructive.[11]

What makes marriage an equal partnership is the manner in which it is lived out, not the manner in which it is structured. Husbands and wives mutually serve one another in love—this is the vast difference having Jesus in our lives makes. "Submit to one another out of reverence for Christ" (Ephesians 5:21).

Christian husbands and wives are called to complementary roles of loving service to each other. Dwight Small said:

> The glory of the woman is the acknowledgment that man is incomplete without her. The humility of the woman is the acknowledgment that she was made for man; the humility of the man is the acknowledgment that he is incomplete without her. Both share an equal dignity, honor and worth.[12]

In his devotional book *Forty Ways to Say I Love You*, James Bjorge sums up the marriage relationship in this way: "Wise partners hang on to one another with open hands so that neither suffocates in submission."[13]

❖ What do you think about James Bjorge's statement?

❖ How might a person feel he or she is suffocating in a marriage?

❖ How does this relate to your relationship?

What is forgiveness? Contrary to what many people think, *forgiveness is not a feeling*. It's a clear and logical *choice* on your part. "Bear with each other and forgive one another if any of you has a grievance against someone. Forgive as the Lord forgave you" (Colossians 3:13).

Forgiveness is not demanding change from your partner before you're willing to consider letting him or her off the hook. Your partner can't guarantee that he or she will never make the same mistake again. Forgiveness means investing trust in your partner. You must give your partner the freedom to fail and grow in your relationship.

Forgiveness *is not* excusing or covering up behavior that is detrimental to the person committing the act or to the one against whom the act is committed. Have you ever said something like, "You know I blew it. What I did was thoughtless and wrong. I'm sorry for what I did. With God's help this is going to be evicted from my life. Will you forgive me?"

Do you ever say something similar to this to one another? "Thank you for asking for forgiveness. Yes, I forgive you!" Do you admit, "I'm in the process of forgiving you. It may take a little time, but it will happen. And I promise I won't use your offense against you"?

❖ When an offense comes up within your marriage, how do you handle it?

❖ What can you do to promote forgiveness and grace in your relationship?

83 How Do You View Sex?

Let's talk about sex and sexuality today.

❖ List three negative and three positives you've felt about human sexuality.

❖ What were your first ideas and feelings about sex? Where did they come from?

❖ As you were growing up, who were your sexual role models? Did they offer healthy or unhealthy views of sexuality?

❖ How did your role models affect your understanding and handling of your own dawning sexuality?

❖ Do you have role models for healthy views of togetherness and sex within marriage now? If yes, how does that couple's relationship affect the way you handle sex within your marriage?

❖ How has your sexual relationship changed since your honeymoon? Do you consider those changes for better or worse? Explain.

❖ How can you improve your sexual relationship?

84   Spiritual Closeness

"I feel awkward talking with my partner about God. I don't know what to say, and I don't want to seem either pious or spiritually ignorant." Have you thought or said this? The following questions will probably require some additional time for reflection and sharing, but it's worth the investment.

❖ When did you first experience closeness with God?
   (Describe how and when this occurred.)

❖ Describe a time when you recognized that the Holy Spirit
   was definitely speaking to you.

❖ What are your mental images of God? Which images do
   you wish would fade away? Which ones would you like to
   be stronger?

❖ If Jesus Christ touched your life and healed you from something right now, what would you want it be?

❖ Which Scriptures have meant the most to you? Explain.

❖ What was the first passage of Scripture you memorized? Do
   you still know it?

Hopefully these questions triggered other topics so your discussions will continue. Once you get started, you'll become much more comfortable with the process.[14]

85 Graciousness

We live in a society that emphasizes self. "Think of yourself first." "Do yourself a favor." "You deserve a break." "You're worth it." But putting yourself first is a reflection of insecurity manifested in self-ishness. Instead, why not emphasize graciousness? According to Merriam-Webster's 11th Collegiate Dictionary, "gracious" means "marked by kindness and courtesy, tact and delicacy, characterized by charm, good taste, and generosity of spirit."

❖ How can you live more graciously with your partner? With others?

It's one thing to hear the phrase, "He's a gracious person," but have you heard the expression, "They have a gracious marriage relationship"? Think about this for a moment.

❖ How can you make your marriage reflect graciousness?

❖ As a couple, what can you do to practice hospitality toward some who need it (even if they don't deserve it)?[15]

"God cannot be tempted by evil, nor does he tempt anyone; but each person is tempted when they are dragged away by their own evil desire and enticed" (James 1:13-14). I'm sure you've heard the expression, "The devil made me do it!" We often laugh when somebody excuses misbehavior with that old line. But deep inside we know that we all have a tendency to project the blame for our sin onto the devil, other people, and even God. Do you find it easy to say, "I'm wrong; I did it; I'm responsible"? Probably not. Few people do, especially to their marriage partners!

Within us is a tendency to respond to life with our old nature. We call this "old nature" the "sin nature," and it's present in *every* person. And sometimes we not only give in to it, but we actually nourish it and give it life and power. The responsibility for our sinful responses is ours alone. We have to shoulder that load because we choose to respond that way. Yes, we have a choice![16]

❖ What temptation does your spouse struggle with the most? How can you help him or her resist temptation?

❖ What is the greatest struggle with sin in your marriage? How can this be overcome?

"Gentle words cause life and health; griping brings discouragement" (Proverbs 15:4 TLB). "How wonderful it is to be able to say the right thing at the right time" (15:23 TLB). God is the model for our communication. He extended Himself to each of us and initiated our contact with Him and with others. He created us to be solitary at times and to need interaction at others. Proverbs 12:18 (TLB) has more advice for us on this subject: "Some people like to make cutting remarks, but the words of the wise soothe and heal."

Consider Dwight Small's insightful comments about communication:

> No amount of communication can make marriage perfect, and therefore we should not expect it. God is perfect, the ideal of Christian marriage is perfect, and the means God puts at the disposal of Christian couples are perfect marriage, [but there is] no perfect communication marriage.[17]

❖ How is the sharing in your relationship?

❖ What words does your partner use that are soothing and healing to you?

❖ How can your communication be improved?

"Where did that thought come from?" If you're like I am, you've asked that question about some thoughts that seem to just pop into your mind. Sometimes, we're not only surprised by the thought, but we're also shocked.

By the time we're adults, we've constructed a fairly good-sized mental filing cabinet. It's filled with beliefs about ourselves, about others, about life, and about God. These are our "core beliefs." Core beliefs are the source of what we believe and how we feel about ourselves. They come from many sources and provide the fuel for many of our thoughts. Our automatic thoughts are based on our core beliefs deep inside. These beliefs have been shaped since childhood by a vast array of family relationships, family patterns, and family rules and influence. Those play major roles in our thought lives and in our marriages. According to Shad Helmstetter in his book *What to Say When You Talk to Yourself*, research indicates that as much as 75 percent of everything we think is negative, counterproductive, and works against us. Most of what we have been influenced by isn't the best.[18]

❖ What are three negative and three positive beliefs you have about yourself?

❖ How do these impact your marriage? (Be specific.)

89 Who Are You?

Have you thought about who you are? Think about it for a minute or two. On what do you base your identity? Do you define yourself by a specific role or by what you do? Do you build who you are on your emotional attachments to people, places, and things? Many people quite typically do this, and that would work fine if life were static, certain, and predictable. But it isn't.

❖ "What and who are you?" Please be specific and detailed.

❖ How much of your identity is related to a person, thing, or situation you've lost?

❖ Think for a minute about these questions and then discuss them.

   Who will I be when I no longer...

   • am a father?

   • am a [insert career/job]?

   • have children living at home?

   • am a family person?

   • am an athlete?

   • hold a particular office in an organization?

If you have no sense of who you are beyond your different roles in life, you've confined yourself to a state of future identity confusion.

❖ If you couldn't define who you are by what you do, how would you describe yourself?

90 Family Loss

Our culture is one that emphasizes gathering. We especially like to accumulate things. Meeting that challenge is seen as a reflection on our abilities and our stations in life. There's no limit to what some people will do in the quest for more stuff. But there's one exception to this quest. We don't like to accumulate losses. We often go to great lengths to avoid them. We'll even deny they're part of life! But loss is part of living on Earth and necessary.

Whenever there's a loss that will be lasting, we need to come to the place of saying goodbye to whom or what it was. Family losses occur in many forms, and for a while as we age, it can feel like we're caught in a vise. We're being squeezed by losses on either side—kids as well as parents. Once more, some losses are predictable, such as children becoming independent, moving out, and establishing their own families. Another example is our own parents aging and dying. The death of a parent at any time is a major loss.

❖ What family losses have you experienced?

❖ Describe the way you grieved.

❖ What other losses might you experience in the next ten years?

❖ Describe one of the happiest times of your life.

❖ What do you think was one of the happiest times for your spouse?

❖ Ask each other, "What would make you happier right now?"

❖ Is your purpose in marriage to please one another?

Gary Thomas, in his book *Sacred Marriage*, wrote:

> The first purpose in marriage—beyond happiness, sexual expression, the bearing of children, companionship, mutual care and provision, or anything else—is to please God. The challenge, of course, is that it is utterly *selfless* living; rather than asking, "What will make me happy?" we are told that we must ask, "What will make God happy?" And just in case we don't grasp it immediately, Paul underscores it a few verses later: "Those who live should no longer live for themselves but for him who died for them and was raised again" (2 Corinthians 5:15).[19]

❖ How can you please God more in your marriage this week?

Anger is a warning sign and a clue to underlying attitudes. It's designed to help us detect improper and potentially destructive attitudes. Anger may be the first emotion we're aware of, but it is rarely the first emotion we experience in a particular situation. The emotions that most frequently precede anger are *fear*, *hurt*, and *frustration*.

Take a sheet of paper of paper and respond in writing to the following questions. Then share your responses with your spouse.

❖ How do you feel about becoming frustrated?

❖ How do you feel about getting angry? (Some people enjoy their frustration and anger because they get an adrenaline rush and feel powerful.)

❖ When you're frustrated, do you want to be in control of your response or to be spontaneous? In other words, do you want to decide what to do or just let your feelings take you where they want to go?

❖ If you want to stay in control, how much time and energy are you willing to spend to make this happen? (For change to occur, the motivational level needs to remain both constant and high.)

There is a reason why God inspired man to write the Scriptures, and why He preserved His words through the centuries for us. *God's guidelines for life are the best.* Regardless of what you may have experienced or been taught, God's plan works. Write out the following verses from the books of Proverbs and Nehemiah on separate index cards and carry them with you so you can work on getting them memorized. They'll help you the next time a situation arises that tries to provoke your anger.

The words of the reckless pierce like swords, but the tongue of the wise brings healing (Proverbs 12:18).

Whoever is patient has great understanding, but one who is quick-tempered displays folly (14:29).

He who is slow to anger has great understanding, but he who is hasty of spirit exposes and exalts his folly (14:29 AMP).

He who is slow to anger is better than the mighty, he who rules his [own] spirit than he who takes a city (16:32 AMP, brackets in original).

Good sense makes a man restrain his anger, and it is his glory to overlook a transgression or an offense (19:11 AMP).

I [Nehemiah] was very angry when I heard their cry and these words. I thought it over and then rebuked the nobles and officials (Nehemiah 5:6-7 AMP, brackets in original).

Here are some more thoughts on anger. Consider what Dr. Willard Harley wrote:

> Anger is the feeling that other people cause your unhappiness, and they'll keep upsetting you until they're punished. They can't be reasoned with. The only thing they understand is pain and personal loss. Once you inflict that punishment, they'll think twice about making you unhappy again!
>
> Anger convinces people that the solution to their trouble is to punish the troublemaker. This emotion overrides intelligence, which knows that punishment usually doesn't solve problems; it only makes the people you punish angry and often causes them to want to inflict punishment on you.
>
> When you become angry with your spouse, you have failed to protect your spouse. Anger, which wants you to hurt the one you love, wins out over intelligence, which wants you to provide your spouse safety and security. When anger wins, romantic love loses.
>
> Anger is deceitful: It lets you forget what really happened. It is also cunning: It tries to convince your intelligence that anger is a correct and appropriate reaction to disappointment.

- What are the most important reasons that (A) you direct angry outbursts toward your spouse?
  (B) Your spouse directs angry outbursts toward you?

- (A) When you direct angry outbursts toward your spouse, what do you typically do? (B) When your spouse directs angry outbursts toward you, what does he/she typically do?

- (A) When you direct angry outbursts toward your spouse, what hurts your spouse the most?
(B) When your spouse directs angry outbursts toward you, what hurts you the most?

- (A) When do you try to control angry outbursts toward your spouse and how do you do it?
(B) When does your spouse try to control angry outbursts toward you, and how does he/she do it?

- If you were to decide that you would never direct another angry outburst toward your spouse, how would you stop this?[20]

94 Are You a Spiritual Person?

Are you spiritual? That's a rather blunt question, but are you? If you answered yes, what do you mean by "being spiritual"? Your answer should actually be quite simple. If you have a desire to know and serve God and want a deeper relationship with Him, that's sufficient.

❖ What do you think God has been saying to you these past few months as an individual? As a couple?

❖ What is your picture of God? How would you describe Him?

These topics and questions can be difficult, but discussing them will draw you closer to God and to one another. [21]

In order for careful listening to occur, you need to be aware of some of the obstacles.

Defensiveness. This is when you're supposed to be listening, but instead you're often busy thinking up a rebuttal, an excuse, or an exception to what your spouse is saying. In doing this, you may miss the primary message and respond defensively. Among the variety of defensive responses, two are:

1. *Perhaps we reach a premature conclusion.* "All right, I know just what you're going to say. We've been through this before, and it's the same old thing."

2. *We may read into his/her words our own expectations or project onto another person what we would say in the same situation.*

Not all defensiveness is spoken out loud. Outwardly we could be agreeing, but inside we're saying just the opposite.

❖ If your spouse confronts you about a behavior or attitude you display that is creating a problem, do you typically accept the criticism or defend yourself?

Let's look at some of the communication guidance found in the Living Bible:

> If you refuse criticism, you will end up in poverty and disgrace; if you accept criticism, you are on the road to fame (Proverbs 13:18).

> Don't refuse to accept criticism; get all the help you can (23:12).

It is a badge of honor to accept valid criticism (25:12).

A man who refuses to admit his mistakes can never be successful. But if he confesses and forsakes them, he gets another chance (28:13).

❖ How will you put these passages into practice within your marriage?

96 Improvements?

Have you ever thought that "nothing can change or improve our relationship"? If so, don't believe it. If you do, it will become a self-fulfilling prophecy. If you or anyone else believes that nothing can improve your marriage, test this belief. Challenge it.

One husband just wanted to be able to have discussions with his wife without defensive arguments that seemed to erupt constantly. He came up with five statements that he could commit to that eased the situation:

1. He chose to believe that his wife wasn't out to get him or simply to argue with him. She might have some good ideas.

2. He committed himself not to interrupt her, not to argue or debate, and not to walk out on her.

3. He would respond to what she said with statements such as: "Really," "That's interesting," "I hadn't considered that," "Tell me more," and "I'd like to think about that."

4. He chose to think the following: *Even if this doesn't work the first time, I'll try it at least five times.*

5. He determined to thank her for each discussion, and when her response was even five percent less defensive, to compliment her for the way she responded.

What about you? What would you like to change? The first step may be to change your beliefs.[22]

❖ What can you do to change the pattern of arguments within your marriage?

97   Guard Your Heart

What do you and your spouse need to do more carefully at this time in your married life?

Years ago people watching television were captivated by the police show *Hill Street Blues*. After their morning briefing and just before they hit the streets, the sergeant would say to the officers, "Let's be careful out there." He was warning them to keep their guard up because the unpredictable could and would happen.

The same caution is repeated throughout the Scriptures for us. Listen to these warnings:

> Be careful to do what is right (Romans 12:17).
>
> Be very careful, then, how you live—not as unwise but as wise (Ephesians 5:15).
>
> Be careful that none of you be found to have fallen short (Hebrews 4:1).
>
> Only be careful, and watch yourselves (Deuteronomy 4:9).
>
> Be careful to do what the LORD your God has commanded you (5:32).
>
> Be careful that you do not forget the LORD (6:12).
>
> Be careful to obey all that is written in the Book of the Law of Moses (Joshua 23:6).
>
> Give careful thought to your ways (Haggai 1:5).

Together, read those eight verses out loud every morning for a month. Before long you'll know them from memory. That's the best safeguard.[23]

❖ What do you need to be more comfortable about guarding your heart, your spouse's heart, and your marriage?

98   Six Styles of Love

People love and express their love in various ways. Are you aware of your particular style? Consider these definitions:

1. *Best Friends Love* style is a comfortable intimacy that develops over a period of time.

2. *Game-Playing Love* is a second style of love. To the game-playing lover, an emotional relationship is a contest to be won.

3. *Logical Love* is a style in which a person concentrates upon the practical values that can be found in the relationship. These people are very pragmatic and often have a list of what they are looking for in a mate. Romance does have some place in the relationship.

4. *Possessive Love* is the most unfulfilling and limiting type of love. The possessive lover has a frantic need to know that he or she is loved.

5. *Romantic Love* is best described as "two people involved in a totally emotional relationship." Romantic lovers are in love with love itself.

6. *Unselfish Love* is a giving, forgiving, unconditionally caring, and nurturing love. Self-sacrifice is involved.

❖ What is your style of love based on the descriptions just given?

Use the following chart to rate yourself on a scale of 0 to 10 (0 means nonexistent, 5 means average, and 10 means very strong). Then do the same for your partner. You may discover that you and/

or your partner are a combination of two or more styles. That is common.

Best Friend Love

1   2   3   4   5   6   7   8   9   10

Game-Playing Love

1   2   3   4   5   6   7   8   9   10

Logical Love

1   2   3   4   5   6   7   8   9   10

Possessive Love

1   2   3   4   5   6   7   8   9   10

Romantic Love

1   2   3   4   5   6   7   8   9   10

Unselfish Love

1   2   3   4   5   6   7   8   9   10[24]

❖ Now go back and mark which one you'd like to develop more in yourself and which one you'd like to see more developed in your spouse.

For more years than I want to admit, I've asked counselees, "If what you're doing in your relationship isn't working, why keep doing it? There's got to be a better way." And so we look for a better way and then implement it in their marriages. You and I want the same thing—to see our marriages grow and reflect our commitment as well as our relationship with the Lord.

Right now your task is to identify and emphasize positive behaviors that will build your marital relationship. The principle behind emphasizing the positive behaviors is that it drowns out the negative. For example, I've had couples tell me that a 45-minute counseling session wouldn't be time enough to tell me all their marital difficulties. However, instead of letting the couple go on and on about their problems, I ask each one to summarize in three minutes what the problems are. Then I ask about the positive benefits, special times, and experiences they appreciate about one another.

What's the result? Many couples realize their marriage is in better shape than they thought. They realize that by just focusing on the negatives, they were ignoring the positives.

❖ What have you been doing that has created positive changes in your marriage?

100   Marriage Is Delicate Yet Resilient

I asked a number of individuals what they have learned about marriage. Here are some of the responses.

- "I've never seen a perfect marriage. It's not something you can package; it's a daily creation."

- "The best description I know of marriage is it's like a child who needs to be picked up and hugged daily and given as much personal attention as possible."

- "Marriage? It's not something simple, and it shouldn't be weighed against your expectations and rejected when they're not met."

- "Since I'm an artist I think the best way to describe it is that every marriage needs a delicate touch and patient treatment."

- "Marriage is like entering a darkened house or a forest where there is no light. To stay safe and make progress, a person needs to move slowly and gently in the dark. The danger is not in the dark. The danger is in losing hope or patience."

❖ List five ways you can "hug" your marriage.

❖ How will you give your marriage "a delicate touch"?

❖ What can your partner do or say to help you maintain your hope and patience?

101   Where Do You Go Now?

Marriage is more than sharing a life together; it's building a life together. What you do now is for sharing and building. What your purpose as a couple is now is to further the kingdom of God and give glory to God. God's Word says:

> Two are better than one, because they have a good return for their labor: If either of them falls down, one can help the other up...Also, if two lie down together, they will keep warm. But how can one keep warm alone? Though one may be overpowered, two can defend themselves. A cord of three strands is not quickly broken (Ecclesiastes 4:9-12).

I'd like to tell you about a friend of mine named Dale. We've been friends for more than forty years. When he was in his early- to mid-forties, Dale began looking for the right woman to marry. He was thoughtful, selective, and had a definite list of criteria that included a strong walk with the Lord. After several years, some of us began wondering if the woman he was looking for *didn't* exist.

But then it happened. At the age of fifty-two, Dale met Sherry, who was thirty-nine. Dale had said he didn't want to marry anyone who had children, but God had other plans. Sherry had three—ages twenty-one, eighteen, and nine. Years later, Dale said he never realized what a great experience he would have being a stepfather. I'll let Dale tell you more of his story.

> My wife and I met through the Internet but really it was through a lot of prayer. God just used that to allow us to find each other. We both had been looking a long time for the right person, but never seemed to find

the "right one." That was, until I got an e-mail from a nurse in San Diego asking to write to her because she thought we might have a number of things in common. I did, and I could tell from her correspondence that her heart was very sincere and that I had found a very special lady.

After writing and talking on the phone for what seemed like weeks, we met in Julian, where she was on a church retreat for the weekend. She proceeded to tell me as we walked and talked, that at the retreat while praying, Jesus told her that I was going to marry her. I looked at her, a little surprised, and told her that He hadn't told me. And she said, "Have you asked Him?"

We had such a great first date that we decided to get together again the next day and go for a walk on the beach. She took me to her favorite beach, Del Mar. After walking for a while, she wanted to show me around other parts of Del Mar, so we continued to walk. We went past beautiful parks, art galleries, food places. Then we came to this beautiful church and walked around, looking at the stained glass, where she told me, "I would love to get married someday in this church." Not realizing that this was the church that she already attended and had so many friends at, I told her, "That's nice." Well, six months later we were married in that church—and yes, Jesus did tell me that she was the one.

So after being single for several years following a marriage that didn't last, Dale remarried and moved into the arena of "we" rather than "me." He shared one of his adjustment experiences.

I was so used to being single, and even being a "married

single" in my first marriage, that I didn't give much regard to someone else when I made decisions. I was on my own. But soon after Sherry and I married, I "just" invited my parents and my brother and his wife over for dinner. I told Sherry they were coming over Friday night, and after a few seconds she said, "Dale, I love your family and certainly want them over, but that won't cut it. We need to talk it over with one another first before we make a decision. I won't refuse you. I just want to be included." I needed to learn that it was now "we" and not "me." My old habits needed to change. And I'm glad I had a wife who would help me make this change. "We" is so much better than "me"!

This was one of many learning experiences that Dale and Sherry navigated well. As I watched them and talked with them, it seemed as though they were on a perpetual honeymoon. They grew together, studied together, worked out together, fished and hunted together. The honeymoon went on for three-and-a-half years. Then Sherry contracted lung cancer, and her health began to go downhill over a period of several months.

Since I'm a trauma crisis counselor, when the tragic terrorist event in New York occurred on September 11, 2001, I was asked to travel to New York to help the survivors. But at God's direction, I remained in California to be with Dale during the last days of Sherry's life. (I later ministered in New York on five separate occasions.)

Just before Sherry died, she wanted to see her black lab, Molly, one more time. So Dale and I marched Molly down the hall of the ICU and put her on the bed. That was a feat in itself, since Molly was ready to deliver eight pups any moment.

The day before she died, Sherry asked all of her friends to come by. What she said to everyone was, "The best thing you can do for

me is to invite Jesus into your life so we can be together in heaven."
Dale asked me to read his eulogy at Sherry's service. Here is a por-
tion of what he'd written:

> From the time Sherry and I first knew that she had
> cancer, she knew she was in a battle for her life, but
> she felt she was in a win–win situation. If she lived,
> she would be able to continue to have a wonderful life
> here on earth; and if she didn't, she would be in heaven
> with her Lord. But she really wanted to live with her
> family. She loved being married, loved me so deeply,
> and wanted to beat this terrible disease so badly that
> she underwent chemotherapy, did all kinds of holis-
> tic medicines, acupuncture, and even had a special
> machine she would use for one hour every night that
> had good results on other types of cancer. She spent a
> long time daily with God, asking Him to heal her if it
> was His will. But God had other plans for her.
>
> What Sherry and I had in three-and-a-half years
> together was packed with so many memories. We
> thought we were making up for things we missed out
> on in the past, but we didn't realize we were doing
> things for the future we wouldn't have together. We
> had a wonderful time and life together. Neither of us
> would have changed it for anything, and I would do
> it over again in a second if God gave me that chance.
> If there is one thing from this that could be passed on
> to any couple, it would be to enjoy every minute you
> have together…as it could be your last.

The psalmist said, "Teach us to number our days, that we may
gain a heart of wisdom" (Psalm 90:12). Your days together are not
limitless. If you can number your days and accept that they are

limited, then perhaps you will learn to protect your time together as a couple. One day there will be just one of you left. You will yearn for more time together, but it will be gone.

Please don't forget my friend Dale's message. I know I won't. I pray that his experience will impact your life and encourage you to cherish your spouse and your marriage.

Notes

Your Marriage Can Be Better Than Ever!

1. Dan Allender and Tremper Longman, *Intimate Allies* (Wheaton, IL: Tyndale House, 1995), 25-30.

2. Ibid., adapted, 30, 34.

#1 Safe Haven – #34 Encouragement

1. Archibald D. Hart, PhD, and Sharon Hart Morris, PhD, *Safe Haven Marriage* (Nashville: Word Publishing Group, 2003), 215.

2. Ibid., 5.

3. Ibid., 11.

4. Ibid., adapted, 19.

5. Ibid., 24.

6. Ibid., adapted, 24.

7. Ibid., adapted, 68-69.

8. Ibid., 74.

9. Ron Peterson, Rutgers University, adapted from his research, quoted in Hart and Hart Morris, *Safe Haven Marriage,* 94.

10. Hart and Hart Morris, *Safe Haven Marriage*, 93-95.

11. Ibid., adapted, 111-12.

12. Scott Stanley, PhD, *The Heart of Commitment* (Nashville: Thomas Nelson Publishers, 1996), adapted, 89-90.

13. Ibid., adapted, 67-83.

14. Ibid., 120.

15. Ibid., adapted, 135.

16. Gregory K. Popcak, MSW, *The Exceptional Seven Percent—The Nine Secrets of the World's Happiest Couples* (New York: Kensington Publishing Group, 2000), 73.

17. Ibid., 76-77.

18. Ibid., 164-69.

19. Ibid.

20. Ibid., adapted, 165.

21. Ibid., 166.

22. Ibid., adapted, 167.

23. Michele Weiner-Davis, *The Divorce Remedy* (New York: Simon & Schuster, 2001), 54-55.

24. Ibid., 95-96.

25. Michele Weiner-Davis, *Divorce Busting* (New York: Summit Books, 1992), adapted, 124-40.

26. John Gottman, PhD, *Why Marriages Succeed or Fail* (New York: Simon & Schuster, 1994), 57.

27. Ibid., adapted, 59-61.

28. David L. Luecke, *The Relationship Manual* (Columbus, MD: The Relationship Institute, 1981), adapted, 65.

29. John M. Gottman, PhD, and Nan Silver, *The Seven Principles for Making Marriage Work* (New York: Harmony, 1999), adapted, 50-51.

30. Ken Gire, *A Reflective Life* (Colorado Springs: Chariot Victor, 1998), 85-86.

31. Rick Warren, *The Purpose Driven Life* (Grand Rapids, MI: Zondervan, 2002), 92-93.

32. Dr. Richard Matteson and James Long Harris, *What If I Married the Wrong Person?* (Minneapolis: Bethany House, 1996), 234-35.

33. Cliff and Joyce Penner, *Men and Sex* (Nashville: Thomas Nelson, 1997), 155-56.

34. Don Dinkmeyer and Lewis Losoncy, *The Encouragement Book* (Englewood Cliffs, NJ: Prentice Hall, 1980), adapted, 50-83.

#35 Reminders – #68 Loss

1. Dr. Wayne Oates.

2. Dr. Robert Shaper, message given at Fuller Theological Seminary, Forest Home Conference Grounds.

3. Dr. David Hubbard, president of Fuller Theological Seminary.

4. Norman H. Wright, *Bringing Out the Best in Your Husband* (Ventura, CA: Regal, 2012), quoting from Cliff and Joyce Penner, *Men and Sex* (Nashville: Thomas Nelson, 1997), 158-81.

5. Emerson Eggerichs, PhD, *Love and Respect* (Colorado Springs: Focus on the Family, 2004), adapted, 38-39.

6. Ibid., adapted, 132, 144.

7. Ibid., 311-12.

8. Gary Rosberg, PhD, and Barbara Rosberg, *6 Secrets to a Lasting Love* (Wheaton, IL: Tyndale House, 2006), 32-35.

9. Gary D. Chapman, PhD, *The Four Seasons of Marriage* (Wheaton, IL: Tyndale House, 2005), 81.

10. Rosberg and Rosberg, *6 Secrets to a Lasting Love*, 222-27.

11. Marcia Lasswell and Norman M. Lobsenz, *No Fault Marriage* (New York: Ballentine Books, 1981), np.

#69 What Bothers You – #101 Where Do You Go Now?

1. Donald R. Harvey, *The Drifting Marriage* (Old Tappan, NJ: Fleming H. Revell, 1988), 123-24.

2. Ibid., 125.

3. Willard F. Harley Jr., *Love Busters* (Tarrytown, NY: Fleming H. Revell, 1992), 138-39.

4. Willard F. Harley Jr. *His Needs, Her Needs* (Tarrytown, NY: Fleming H. Revell, 2001), adapted, 125-26.

5. Ibid., adapted, 130-31.

6. Ibid., adapted, 130-31.

7. Ibid., adapted, 130-31.

8. Ron Deal and David Olson, *The Remarriage Checkup* (Minneapolis: Bethany House, 2010), 186-89.

9. Clifford Notarius, PhD, and Howard Markman, PhD, *We Can Work It Out* (New York: G.P. Putnam's Sons, 1995), adapted, 70-75.

10. Harley Jr., *His Needs, Her Needs*, 66.

11. Ibid., adapted, 80-83.

12. Dwight Small, *Christian, Celebrate Your Sexuality* (Old Tappan, NJ: Fleming H. Revell, 1974), 144.

13. James Bjorge, *Forty Ways to Say I Love You* (Minneapolis: Augsburg Publishers, 1978), 20.

14. Paul Stevens, *Marriage Spirituality* (Downers Grove, IL: InterVarsity Press, 1989), adapted, 50-52.

15. Peter Lord, *Hearing God* (Grand Rapids, MI: Baker Book House, 1990), adapted, 152-54.

16. Gene Getz, *Believing God When You Are Tempted to Doubt* (Ventura, CA: Regal Books, 1985), adapted, 66-70.

17. Dwight H. Small, *After You've Said I Do* (Minneapolis: Augsburg Publications, 1978), 20.

18. Shad Helmstetter, *What to Say When You Talk to Yourself* (New York: Pocket Books, 1982), adapted, 20-24.

19. Gary Thomas, *Sacred Marriage* (Grand Rapids, MI: Zondervan, 2002), 33.

20. Harley Jr., *Love Busters*, 28, 30-31.

21. Peter Lord, *Helping God* (Grand Rapids, MI: Baker Book House, 1990), adapted, 152-54.

22. Ibid., 99-101.

23. William and Kristi Gaultiere, *Mistaken Identity* (Old Tappan, NJ: Fleming H. Revell, 1989), adapted, 99.

24. Marcia Lasswell and Norman L. Lobenz, *Styles of Loving: Why You Love the Way You Do* (New York: Doubleday and Co., Inc., 1981), adapted, 167-68.

Great Harvest House Books by
H. Norman Wright

101 Ways to Build a Stronger, More Exciting Marriage

101 Questions to Ask Before You Get Engaged

101 Questions to Ask Before You Get Remarried

After You Say "I Do"

Before You Remarry

Before You Say "I Do"®

Coping with Chronic Illness

Finding the Life You've Been Looking For

Finding the Right One for You

Helping Your Kids Deal with Anger, Fear, and Sadness

Quiet Times for Couples (Devotional)

Quiet Times for Parents (Devotional, ebook only)

Quiet Times for Those Who Need Comfort (Devotional, ebook only)

Reflections of a Grieving Spouse

Strong to the Core (Devotional)

Success over Stress

Truly Devoted (Dogs)

What to Say When You Don't Know What to Say

Winning over Your Emotions

Quiet Times for Couples

*"Let Norman Wright guide you together to God...
and your marriage will never be the same."*

MAX LUCADO

**Uplifting, insightful devotions that will inspire,
encourage, and strengthen your marriage**

In these short devotions that promote togetherness, joy, and sharing your dreams, trusted Christian counselor and bestselling author Norm Wright offers...

- innovative ideas to establish and maintain a flourishing marriage
- insights for encouraging intimacy and harmony
- little and big things you can do to enhance your relationship
- specific suggestions for accommodating differences and handling conflicts
- great ideas for supporting and helping your spouse

Your relationship will become more loving, considerate, and united as the two of you experience these quiet "together times" filled with deep insights, powerful meditations, God's presence, and His truths and love.

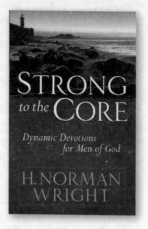

Strong to the Core

Strengthen Your Heart, Mind, and Spirit
in Just 5 Minutes a Day

Bestselling author Norm Wright has a proven plan to help you strengthen your core—your spiritual life, your family life, and your personal life. In these short devotions you'll find biblical truth, wisdom for growing your relationships, and time-tested advice for handling temptations and working through problems.

Professional knowledge coupled with practical insights garnered through Norm's many years as a respected Christian counselor will help you...

- increase your understanding of the Lord and His will
- communicate more effectively in relationships, especially marriage
- strengthen your reliance on God and His Word
- develop traits that reveal your heart for God
- implement your faith and God-given gifts to help others

Strong to the Core encourages you to embrace God's call to live for Him, represent Him, and take a stand for Him. You can make a difference!

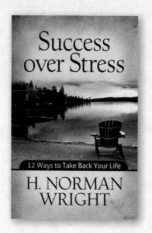

Success over Stress

Isn't it time to take back your life?

You can't eliminate all stress, but you can certainly lessen its negative impact. Noted Christian counselor Norm Wright shares the action steps that have enabled thousands of people to find greater happiness, satisfaction, and peace. Through true, encouraging stories, biblical wisdom, and practical suggestions, you'll discover how to decrease your stressors by:

- simplifying your work and home life
- releasing any emotional baggage
- taking control of your schedule and finances
- establishing livable goals and priorities
- experiencing God's presence more fully

Packed with sound advice and proven steps for handling worry, fear, irritation, and more, *Success over Stress* reveals how you can experience more joy, energy, and satisfaction every day.